THE

GHIRARDELLI
CHOCOLATE COOKBOOK

Recipes and History from America's Premier Chocolate Maker

Photography by Leigh Beisch

TEN SPEED PRESS
Berkeley

All rights reserved. Published in the United States by Ten Speed Press, an imprint of the Crown Publishing Group, a division of Random House, Inc., New York.
www.crownpublishing.com
www.tenspeed.com

Ten Speed Press and the Ten Speed Press colophon are registered trademarks of Random House, Inc.

Library of Congress Cataloging-in-Publication Data
The Ghirardelli cookbook : recipes and history from America's premier
chocolate maker / By The Ghirardelli Chocolate Company.
        p. cm.
   Includes index.
  1. Cookery (Chocolate) 2. Chocolate desserts. I. Ghirardelli Chocolate
Company.
  TX767.C5G57 2007
  641.3'374—dc22

                              2007018171

ISBN 978-1-58008-871-8
Printed in China

Cover and text design by Ed Anderson
Food Styling by Merilee Bordin
Prop Styling by Emma Star Jensen
Food Stylist Assistant: Nan Bullock
Photography Assistant: Lauren Grant

14 13 12 11 10 9 8 7 6 5

Second Edition

THE GHIRARDELLI

CHOCOLATE COOKBOOK

CONTENTS

Preface 7

Introduction

    The Legendary Story of Ghirardelli 10

    From Bean to Bar 14

    Chocolate Primer 17

    Savoring Chocolate with All Your Senses 21

    Entertaining with Chocolate 23

Chocolate Cookies 26

Chocolate Brownies and Bars 50

Chocolate Cakes, Cupcakes, and Tortes 62

Chocolate Pies, Tarts, and Other Spectacular Desserts 88

Chocolate Candies and Bonbons 116

Chocolate Breads and Breakfast 134

Anything-but-Boring Chocolate Drinks 144

Acknowledgments 153

Glossary 154

Index 156

PREFACE

Since the launch of the Ghirardelli Chocolate Company's last cookbook in the mid-nineties, the premium chocolate market in America—both in confections and baking—has evolved and grown tremendously, especially in the increasing sophistication and demands of consumers for higher-quality chocolate products. We invite you to use this book to experiment with the different grades and flavors of chocolate, from extra bitter to creamy milk chocolate.

Everyone has a favorite way to enjoy chocolate, whether it's snatching a handful of a favorite treat from the candy dish at work or savoring a sliver of dark, bitter chocolate after a long day. Chocolate also lends itself brilliantly to baking and is easily transformed into a gourmet dessert—whether a simple fondue or an extravagent layered torte. Once reserved only for special occasions, premium chocolate has gradually become a staple that provides delight for everyday life.

The recipes in this cookbook range from simple to complex and include everyday recipes and recipes perfect for celebrations. The recipes come from our own chocolate masters at Ghirardelli and Ghirardelli aficionados, the winner of the Ghirardelli "Is Your Dessert Intense Enough" national baking contest, and renowned pastry chefs from the San Francisco Bay Area, where the Ghirardelli Chocolate Company is rooted. Each sweet dessert uses premium Ghirardelli baking chocolates, which are available at grocery, specialty, and mass merchandisers nationwide.

GHIRARDELLI'S *Ground* CHOCOLAT

YOUR **GUEST** DESERVES THE BEST!

INTRODUCTION

THE LEGENDARY STORY OF GHIRARDELLI

Our intense chocolate journey begins with the legendary story of Domingo Ghirardelli, a young Italian apprentice who followed his sweet dreams to San Francisco.

HUMBLE BEGINNINGS

The story of Domingo Ghirardelli doesn't start in the renowned hills of San Francisco, where the famed Ghirardelli Chocolate Company began. It begins, rather, in another hill town, in the north of Italy where a young Ghirardelli studied as a fledgling chocolatier at the age of eleven.

In 1828, in Rapallo, Italy, a small Ligurian hill town just near Genoa, Ghirardelli started his apprenticeship with a Genoan master chocolatier. From making premium chocolate delicacies, sugar loaves, and Italian fudgelike candies, to crafting other sweet confections, Ghirardelli was able to learn about the intricate steps of fine chocolate making under Signor Romanengo.

But thoughts of sweet treats were nothing new to Ghirardelli, whose father, an exotic foods importer, brought tales of Ceylon, Sumatra, and Peru into the imagination of this adventurous youth. Practically smelling the exotic spices and adventure, Ghirardelli set sail at age twenty. He was off to Montevideo, Uruguay, with his young wife, Elisabetta, or Bettina as he fondly called her. He planned to make his own adventures and work in the coffee and spice business. The New World attracted many European entrepreneurs, and Ghirardelli and other Italians were drawn to Uruguay because of the well-matched Latin culture.

From Uruguay, the family moved to Peru, where there was rumored to be more work for ambitious, young, and hard-working men. Lima, Peru was thriving economically from a flush of worldwide exports commerce, and the young Ghirardelli family wanted to be a part of this prosperous time. After only a year in Uruguay, they packed their bags and settled in Lima, opening a small store on the main shopping boulevard, selling confections and specializing in chocolate.

But stories have their ups and downs, and heroes are rarely without their own hardships to overcome. Despite immediate success upon opening the shop and settling into the new surroundings, young Bettina died shortly after the couple arrived in Peru. Ghirardelli remarried to the widow Carmen Alvarado, supporting her and his new stepdaughter, coincidentally named Dominga.

Ghirardelli and his new family moved into a small building next door to James Lick, a piano maker and cabinetmaker from the U.S. Both were enterprising young foreigners, both adventurous, and both looking for the next great opportunity; they became fast friends.

News was traveling fast through the Americas that the newest business hotspot was in the western part of North America. Over the next year, Ghirardelli and James sold their businesses and packed for their next adventure—California. In 1848, James put down roots in the California territory of Yerba Buena, specifically

San Francisco. Ghirardelli sent him 600 pounds of chocolate to see how it would sell, and the answer was "tremendously." Two weeks after James landed, gold was discovered, and the luxurious chocolate sold out quickly.

The two friends corresponded by letter, James waxing on the amazing opportunities and urging Ghirardelli to move quickly and bring more chocolate. So he did, leaving his wife and now three children in Peru to remain until he got settled. He arrived in California on February 24, 1849, just days before American ships started arriving from the East Coast with gold-seeking prospectors.

DIGGING FOR GOLD

It was the end of 1849, and San Francisco's population was on the rise, reaching 25,000 in a very short time. Like most immigrants, Ghirardelli tried his hand at prospecting, but instead found himself focusing his attention on the trade that he knew and loved. He opened a tent store in Stockton, California, east of San Francisco, to sell supplies to the miners. Miners were coming into the store with gold dust twinkling in their eyes, and Ghirardelli offered them necessary tools, coffee, spices, and, of course, chocolate.

The success of this first store led to a second in San Francisco, which was just as well received. Ghirardelli had his hand in many golden pots—grubstaking, stores, a French soda fountain, and The Europa, one of San Francisco's first hotels. In 1850, California was admitted as a state. By then, the population of flourishing San Francisco encompassed an additional 10,000 citizens, and by 1855, it had risen to over 50,000.

THE GREAT FIRES AND THE GHIRARDELLI CHOCOLATE COMPANY

The Gold Rush forced the quick development of Northern California. Then, the fires started, and San Francisco was shaken. After two major fires in 1850, the San Francisco Fire Department was formed, but despite this measure, fires continued to devastate the city. On May 4, 1851, a fifth "great fire" ripped through Portsmouth Square, destroying more than two thousand buildings and resulting in over $5 million in damages. Ghirardelli's store and hotel were razed by the fire. Three days later, an unrelated but equally unfortunate fire leveled Ghirardelli's Stockton outlet.

Burned out but not dejected, Ghirardelli recouped enough capital and spirit to open a coffee and confectionary shop on Commercial Street in San Francisco. After a year, he moved to a larger and better-situated location on the corner of Washington and Kearny streets and opened what would soon become the Ghirardelli Chocolate Company.

In 1852, Ghirardelli incorporated, and he was finally able to bring his wife and children over to their new home from Lima to help start this multigenerational company.

PERFECTING CHOCOLATE MAKING

The Ghirardelli Chocolate Company dealt solely in imports and purchased goods until 1855, when they upgraded to another, larger location at Greenwich and Powell streets. Ghirardelli wanted to manufacture his own chocolate, but to do so, he had to import large machinery from Peru and Switzerland.

The business was thriving, and Ghirardelli opened several more stores—in Oakland, Stockton, and Sonora.

He brought in partners and family members to help run the businesses.

Chocolate consumption was on the rise, and consumers were looking for new ways to enjoy this treat.

In 1867, Ghirardelli discovered the Broma process, which is still used today. A bag of ground cocoa beans was left hanging in a warm room for a prolonged period, and the resulting mess—cocoa butter dripping out onto the floor—was a revelation. The cocoa left in the sack was almost completely devoid of cocoa fat and was soon made into the base of Ghirardelli's Sweet Ground Chocolate and Cocoa—a product that, with few modifications, is still widely consumed. This was sweet news for a rapidly growing business.

RECESSION AND RECOVERY

Even with the discoveries bringing new life to the business, a depression hit in the late nineteenth century, and Ghirardelli, like many other businesses, wasn't spared. The company filed for bankruptcy in 1870, and Ghirardelli turned over some businesses and personal assets. But with time, the debts were paid with earnings from the sale of everything but the plant in San Francisco, and Ghirardelli took advantage of the burgeoning industrial revolution.

Fast rail transportation allowed for quicker and expanded distribution of Ghirardelli's products from California to the East Coast, which was once accessible only by ship. With more consumers came more innovation, and the Ghirardelli Chocolate Company began to offer new flavors, including the Swiss-inspired creamy milk chocolate.

In 1892, Domingo Ghirardelli officially retired, handing over his chocolate empire and presidency to his eldest son, Domingo, Jr.

While his son took the reins, increasing advertising and promotions, the senior Ghirardelli traveled. During a visit to his hometown of Rapallo, Italy, he quietly passed away on January 17, 1894.

THE FAMED GHIRARDELLI SQUARE

With Domingo, Jr. increasing the size of the company and the product line, naturally they needed more space. After several moves, the company settled for a beautiful space on North Point overlooking the San Francisco Bay. In 1906, earthquakes and fires ravaged San Francisco, but the Ghirardelli complex remained intact. More buildings were erected in 1910, including the Mustard Works, Chocolate Building, Cocoa Building, and Power House, with the stately Clock Tower at the corner of Larkin and North Point Streets crowning the site. Ghirardelli Square was established, becoming one of the most notable landmarks in San Francisco. In 1923, the famed fifteen-foot Ghirardelli sign lit the buildings for the first time over the square.

DURING THE WAR

In the early years of World War II, the Ghirardelli sign was darkened to accommodate the city's blackouts, but the enthusiasm of the San Francisco company did not dim as employees rallied together to ship much-needed chocolate bars to the nation's troops. Additionally, Ghirardelli started packing what little cocoa was available (sugar and cocoa beans proving difficult to import at wartime) in "Victory Packs," which were designed to conserve precious metal.

In the early 1960s, San Francisco-based Golden Grain Macaroni Company bought the Ghirardelli Chocolate Company and in the process moved the headquarters out of the city to San Leandro. William Roth and his mother, two prominent San Franciscans, bought Ghirardelli Square, saving it from the fate of being converted to apartment buildings. Instead, the area was built up with boutiques, and today there are more than forty shops and restaurants. In 1965 Ghirardelli Square was declared an official city landmark; in 1982, it became a national historic landmark.

THE NEW FACE OF GHIRARDELLI

After Golden Grain, the company changed hands several more times before being bought in 1998 by Lindt and Sprüngli AG, the Swiss-based leaders in premium chocolate manufacturing.

In the late 1990s, and continuing to present time, newer, more modern chocolate manufacturing equipment produced new flavors and textures. In 2002, the Ghirardelli Chocolate Company celebrated the 150th anniversary of Mr. Domingo Ghirardelli's legacy of premium chocolate manufacturing in America.

Today, Ghirardelli continues to shape the increasingly sophisticated tastes of chocolate consumers in America by continually developing new flavors—from intense, rich dark chocolates, to velvety, creamy white chocolates. And Ghirardelli chocolates are still made with the passion that Ghirardelli himself brought to the original product. Though long gone, that visionary Italian chocolate maker would approve.

A TASTE OF CHOCOLATE HISTORY

Historians can't pinpoint exactly when chocolate was first invented, but the Mayans of the Yucatan first cultivated the cacao bean.

The cacao tree, known as Theobroma cacao, is native to the tropical rainforests of the Americas and is believed to have spread northward through Mexico. The Aztec people adopted chocolate for use in a rich, dense drink called xocolatl, or "bitter water," enjoyed by their Emperor Montezuma II. Chocolate was said to give energy and wisdom. It was thought to be an aphrodisiac and was linked to the fertility goddess.

In the sixteenth century, Montezuma shared the drink, most likely spiked with vanilla, cinnamon, and achiote, with Spanish explorer and conquistador Hernán Cortés. Enamored with this drink, he brought cacao beans back to his native Spain where it became a popular luxury item. And thus began Europe's love affair with chocolate.

It took one hundred years for other European countries to catch on, but when they did, consumers in France, Italy, and the Netherlands began to enjoy chocolate as a beverage. They began adding another luxury item—sugar—making the drink sweeter, richer, and generally more delicious. In the mid-1600s, chocolate houses, lounges where noblemen enjoyed chocolate drinks, began opening around Europe. By the 1700s, chocolate was being mass produced, making it affordable to common citizens.

Until around 1900, Europeans and Americans imported their cacao beans mainly from South America, Central America, and the West Indies. At the beginning of the twentieth century, the growing conditions in West Africa proved remarkably sympathetic to the temperamental needs of the cocoa tree, and cultivation of the tree spread, reaching unprecedented levels. Today, West African countries supply most of the world's cacao beans, but many companies, including Ghirardelli, use proprietary blends of beans from different nations to create signature flavors.

FROM BEAN TO BAR

Long before a customer can walk into a candy store to buy a chocolate bar and before a chef whips melted chocolate into a silky soufflé, chocolate production starts with a bean. Each part of the process, from growing to processing, alters the flavor of the bean. Ghirardelli is one of few companies worldwide that controls all aspects of chocolate making, starting with bean selection and finishing with the complete manufacturing of and packaging of highly sophisticated chocolate products.

THE SUPREME BEAN

Exceptional chocolate starts with exceptional cacao fruits, leathery pods filled with a sweet pulp in which the beans are embedded. Although they turn a rich brown, the beans are light pink or purple before fermentation.

Trees grow in South America, especially in Brazil and Venezuela, and Central America and in the Caribbean, West Africa, and Southeast Asia, basically anywhere that has hot, wet, tropical weather. Each region produces cacao beans with different and unique flavors, and the varieties of beans can be classified within three different categories:

Forastero: The pods from forastero trees make up most of the cacao harvest, supplying more than 80 percent or more of the world's production. The trees are hearty, plentiful, and easy to cultivate. The bean has a pungent aroma and provides great body to the finished product. This is, by far, the most plentiful type of cacao.

Criollo: The criollo tree is more delicate and less resistant than the heartier forastero. The beans are lighter in color and are highly prized for their spicier, intense flavor. They are considered by many to be the premium bean, and the best are said to come from Venezuela.

Trinitario: This species is a cross between the forastero and criollo trees, which cross-pollinated by accident in Trinidad. The beans have a good, aromatic flavor.

Although there are single varietal chocolates available on the market, more often, beans are carefully selected and blended. The quest for selecting the perfect beans is complicated by the sometimes primitive methods in which cacao beans are harvested, fermented, and dried in their native countries. Each part of the process can alter the flavors of the beans, as can weather conditions, so stringent inspection is vital to ensure the consistent delivery of high-quality product.

At Ghirardelli, the key to making a great chocolate is to carefully select the best beans from the finest regions of the world and masterfully blend them together to create a unique flavor profile. To ensure a consistent delivery of superior-quality chocolate, Ghirardelli experts reject 30 to 40 percent of cacao beans presented to them. Ghirardelli's proprietary blend of cacao beans is refined with more than 150 years of chocolate-making expertise to combine the unique flavor notes characteristic of beans from three regions of the world. This legendary proprietary blend is at the heart of Ghirardelli's distinctive and rich chocolate taste.

PERFECTING CHOCOLATE MAKING

The chocolate makers at Ghirardelli follow four steps to create its signature cocoa and other chocolate products: roasting and pressing, refining, conching, and tempering.

Roasting and Pressing

Unlike many other chocolate manufacturers, Ghirardelli roasts the nibs to achieve its legendary robust and intense chocolate flavor. Raw beans come in from around the world and first pass through a cleaning machine. The beans are heated and vibrated to remove the shell. Only the nibs are left, which are roasted for different lengths of time and temperatures depending on the chocolate flavors being manufactured.

The nibs are milled, or ground, until they liquefy. This is called "chocolate liquor," and it is the essence of pure chocolate.

Chocolate liquor is made into cocoa powder by removing the cocoa butter, using a press or the Broma process, or it is molded, then set into unsweetened chocolate.

Refining

The refining process is one of the most important parts of the manufacturing process and the one that differentiates one chocolate maker from another. At Ghirardelli, chocolatiers add sugar and milk powder, if making milk chocolate, in varying amounts to the chocolate liquor and cocoa butter. All of the ingredients are blended together in large mixers to form a doughlike product. This dough is then sent through the refiners— a set of large rollers that crush the chocolate into tiny flakes around eighteen microns large. This contrasts remarkably with some nonpremium brands, which can have particle sizes up to fifty microns—the diameter of a strand of human hair—leaving a noticeably grainy or gritty texture.

Conching

As the cacao beans finally near their transformation to chocolate, they are sent to large machines, or conches, where they are constantly agitated and kept in a liquid state for a specific length of time. The chocolate is swept back and forth with large paddles for several hours up to several days, until any harsh flavor notes are removed, leaving just a smooth, rounded flavor. Some of Ghirardelli's products with higher cacao contents are conched for lengths of time that are virtually unheard of in the industry. The result of this lengthy conching is products that deliver an intense chocolate taste— without harsh flavor notes.

Tempering

After the conching stage, the chocolate is tempered, a process of heating and cooling the chocolate to create small, stable cocoa butter crystals in the chocolate mass. The mass is deposited into molds, and when done correctly, this stage creates a finished product with a glossy, smooth appearance.

Finally, after the chocolate has been sent through cooling tunnels to solidify the mass, it is packaged in Ghirardelli-designed containers and wrappers, and shipped nationwide to various distribution centers and retailers to ultimately be enjoyed by consumers.

CHOCOLATE VARIETIES

Cacao content refers to everything derived from the cacao bean—chocolate liquor, cocoa butter, and cocoa powder. The cacao content gives an indication of how intense or how sweet the chocolate will be. For example, a chocolate product touting a "60% Cacao" label indicates that 60 percent of the product consists of any combination of cocoa butter and chocolate liquor, with the remaining 40 percent made up of sugar, vanilla, and other ingredients. The preference for a higher cacao content may vary from person to person, or from time to time. More is not always better. When it comes to cacao percentage, finding the perfect balance to suit individual taste is more important than finding the highest percentage available.

In the United States, a set of federal regulations, called the Standards of Identity, govern the composition and nomenclature of chocolate. Chocolate can be legally defined to fit into one of the different chocolate categories defined below.

Unsweetened Chocolate (100 percent cacao content): Unsweetened chocolate is also called chocolate liquor. It is made from finely ground roasted cocoa nibs and can be natural or Dutch-processed (alkalized). Unsweetened chocolate is used in cakes, brownies, and cookies, with the addition of sugar.

Bittersweet Chocolate (35 to 99 percent cacao content): Many types and brands of chocolate fit into this category. Bittersweet chocolate must contain at least 35 percent unsweetened chocolate and less than 12 percent milk solids. Generally, bittersweet chocolate has an unsweetened chocolate content of 50 percent or more.

Semi-Sweet Chocolate (35 to 45 percent cacao content): A variation of bittersweet chocolate, semi-sweet chocolate contains 35 to 45 percent unsweetened chocolate. This chocolate is most typically eaten out of hand or used in baking.

Sweet Chocolate (15 to 34 percent cacao content): Sweet chocolate contains at least 15 percent unsweetened chocolate and less than 12 percent milk solids. Sweet chocolate is also called dark chocolate or plain chocolate.

Milk Chocolate: Milk chocolate contains at least 10 percent unsweetened chocolate, 12 percent milk solids, and 3.39 percent milk fat.

White Chocolate: Previously there were no legal standards to define white chocolate, but that's changed under the Standards of Identity, which now define it as containing at least 20 percent cocoa butter, 14 percent milk solids, and 3 1/2 percent milk fat.

CHOCOLATE PRIMER: STORAGE AND USE

Once you buy your chocolate, proper handling will ensure its shelf life and give you the best products.

STORING CHOCOLATE

To store chocolate, be sure to wrap it tightly and keep it in a cool, dry place with little humidity. In hot climates or during the warm summer months, chocolate can be stored in the refrigerator, although this is not ideal.

If chocolate gets too warm during storage, cocoa butter could appear on the surface, causing the chocolate to develop a gray or white cast, known as bloom. This transformation, however, does not affect the flavor of the chocolate nor its interior color.

Blooming of chocolate products is an unappealing but common problem, and there are two forms of bloom: fat bloom and sugar bloom. Fat bloom is the visible accumulation of large cocoa butter crystals on the surface of the chocolate. It is often accompanied by numerous minute cracks that dull the appearance of chocolate. This might make the chocolate feel slightly oily or melt upon touch. Sugar bloom is the crystallization of sugar, which is often caused by high humidity and the formation of condensate ("sweating") when a cold product is brought into a warm area; this feels grainy to the touch.

To prevent bloom, it is important not to expose chocolate to wide fluctuations in temperature; instead, make all temperature changes gradually. Although it may look unpleasant, bloomed chocolate is not harmful to eat.

MELTING CHOCOLATE

Chocolate will melt quickly and evenly when broken into small pieces, about 1 inch in size. Carefully use a sharp knife to cut baking bars, or use your fingers to break the bars into pieces. Refrigerating chocolate for about 30 minutes will make it easier to break or chop.

Chocolate melts at very low temperatures. It is important to be patient and use low heat because chocolate that is overheated can seize, becoming stiff and grainy.

Do not let any liquid touch the chocolate. Just a few drops of water may also cause the chocolate to seize. Be sure all utensils and containers are thoroughly dry before using them with chocolate.

Double-Boiler (Indirect-Heat) Method
Using indirect heat guarantees the best results for melting chocolate. If you do not own a double boiler, use a glass or metal mixing bowl on top of a saucepan. Fill the bottom of a double boiler, or a saucepan, with enough water to barely touch the bottom of the upper container. Heat the water, but don't let it boil. Place the chocolate chips or broken chocolate in the top of the double boiler or in a heatproof bowl set over the hot water, and stir the chocolate occasionally until it's melted.

Microwave Method

Using a microwave is an easy and effective way to melt chocolate, but microwaves vary greatly in the intensity and evenness of the heat, so you may have to experiment to find the best setting. Using a microwave-safe container, heat the chocolate in a microwave at 50 percent power (medium) for 1 minute. Remove and stir until the bowl no longer feels warm, then continue heating at 15- to 30-second intervals, taking out the chocolate to stir until smooth.

Direct-Heat Method

Use this method when adding chocolate to a batter. Do not use this method for chocolate that will be used for dipping or molding.

Put the chocolate in a heavy saucepan over the lowest possible heat and stir constantly to avoid scorching. Remove the saucepan from the heat when small lumps of chocolate remain, and stir to complete the melting.

TEMPERING CHOCOLATE

Tempering is a method of heating and cooling chocolate to give it a smooth and glossy finish in order to use it for coating or dipping. The tempered chocolate will have a crisp snap, and it will not melt on your fingers as easily.

Tempering Method

There are several ways to temper chocolate, but this is the easiest. Grate or chop the chocolate into small pieces. Place two-thirds of the chocolate in the top of a double boiler. Heat over hot, but not boiling, water, and stir constantly until the chocolate reaches 110° to 115°F on a candy thermometer. Remove the pan with the chocolate in it, and let cool at room temperature until 95° to 100°F. Add the remaining one-third chocolate and stir until melted. The chocolate is now ready to be used for molding candies, coating, or dipping.

TIPS FOR TEMPERING

· Do not heat the chocolate above 130°F since chocolate, especially milk chocolate, is very sensitive to heat and will scorch or seize easily.

· Be sure no liquid gets into the chocolate as this will cause clumping or seizing.

CANDY MAKING AND DIPPING

You will get the best results if you consume the chocolate within two days of melting.

Using the Double-Boiler (Indirect-Heat) Method, Microwave Method, or Tempering Method, heat any of our Ghirardelli chocolate chips or bars until completely melted and smooth. Do not thin the chocolate with water, milk, margarine, or butter.

Dipping

Dip your favorite fruit, candy, pretzels, nuts, or cookies in melted chocolate, place on a tray or baking sheet covered with parchment, then refrigerate for 15 minutes or until firm.

Candy Making

Spoon melted chocolate into candy molds and refrigerate for at least 2 hours or until solid.

GARNISHING PASTRIES WITH CHOCOLATE

A drizzle of chocolate, a chocolate curl, or a beautiful, delicate-looking chocolate leaf can transform any dessert from ordinary to extraordinary.

Chocolate Curls and Shavings

To make chocolate curls, use any four-ounce bar of Ghirardelli chocolate. To make large curls, melt the chocolate in the top of a double boiler or in a heatproof bowl set over barely simmering water. Find a flat surface, such as an upside down baking sheet or a smooth marble cutting board. Spread the melted chocolate evenly onto the flat surface; the chocolate should be the thickness of a butter knife blade. Refrigerate for 10 minutes, or until the chocolate is firm, but not brittle. Hold a metal spatula upside down and press firmly into the chocolate, then push steadily ahead until a curl forms. With a toothpick or a small skewer, carefully lift each curl and place it on the dessert, or store the curls on a plate in the refrigerator until needed.

To make small curls, let the chocolate bar stand in a warm place, such as in the sun or near a lamp, until thoroughly warm but not melted. Holding the chocolate in one hand with a paper towel, or a bit of plastic wrap, make curls using a vegetable peeler drawing the peeler along the thin, flat side of the bar. Remove each curl with a toothpick and place it on the dessert, or store the curls on a plate in the refrigerator until needed.

To make shavings, proceed as directed for small curls but use a short stroke when peeling. For a more splintered effect, use cool rather than warmed chocolate. Both shavings and splinters work best when made directly over the dessert being decorated. Practice first over a plate.

Drizzling or Piping Chocolate

For drizzling chocolate, you will need a pastry bag fitted with a small tip. If you don't have a pastry bag, you can substitute a plastic bag.

To generously drizzle a dessert with chocolate, melt 2 ounces of chocolate in the top of a double boiler or in a heatproof bowl set over barely simmering water until the chocolate has melted, stirring occasionally until smooth. Remove the chocolate from the heat and spoon it into the prepared pastry bag or plastic bag. If using a plastic bag, cut a small opening at a corner of the bottom. The size of the tip or the cut-out determines the thickness of the piping. Gently squeeze the pastry bag to drizzle the dessert with melted chocolate.

CHOCOLATE SUBSTITUTIONS

When you are baking and need to substitute one chocolate product for another, try these options:

Ghirardelli (60% Cacao) Bittersweet Chocolate, (70% Cacao) Extra Bittersweet Chocolate, and Semi-Sweet Chocolate can be used interchangeably.

Ghirardelli Unsweetened Chocolate and Ghirardelli Semi-Sweet Chocolate baking bars: 4 ounces of Ghirardelli Semi-Sweet Chocolate is equivalent to 2 ounces of Ghirardelli Unsweetened Chocolate combined with 1/4 cup of granulated sugar.

Ghirardelli Unsweetened Cocoa and Ghirardelli Sweet Ground Chocolate & Cocoa: For each 1/2 cup of Unsweetened Cocoa, use 1 cup of Sweet Ground Chocolate & Cocoa and decrease the amount of sugar the recipe calls for by 1/2 cup. For recipes that call for 1 cup Ghirardelli Sweet Ground Chocolate & Cocoa, use 1/2 cup Unsweetened Cocoa and 1/2 cup sugar. Mix together prior to adding to the recipe.

Ghirardelli Unsweetened Chocolate and Ghirardelli Unsweetened Cocoa: For every 1 ounce of Unsweetened Chocolate called for in a recipe, use 3 level tablespoons of Unsweetened Cocoa and 1 tablespoon more of butter, margarine, or vegetable shortening than called for in the recipe.

Ghirardelli Sweet Ground Chocolate & Cocoa and Ghirardelli Unsweetened Baking Chocolate: For every 1 ounce of Ghirardelli Unsweetened Baking Chocolate, use 6 level tablespoons of Sweet Ground Chocolate & Cocoa; add 1 tablespoon more of butter, margarine, or vegetable shortening than called for in the recipe; and decrease the amount of sugar the recipe calls for by 3 level tablespoons.

MEASUREMENTS

When your baking calls for chocolate, you may find that outside of this cookbook, some recipes call for 1 cup of baking chips, or maybe 1 bag, or even 6 ounces of a chocolate baking bar. Whatever the case, read on below for our chocolate measurement conversions.

2 cups chocolate chips	1 (12 ounce) bag Ghirardelli Semi-Sweet Chocolate Chips, 1 (11.5 ounce) bag Ghirardelli Milk Chocolate Chips, 1 (11.5 ounce) bag Ghirardelli 60% Cacao Bittersweet Chocolate Chips, or 1 (11 ounces) bag Ghirardelli Classic White Chips
1 cup chocolate chips	$^1/_2$ (12 ounce) bag Ghirardelli Semi-Sweet Chocolate Chips, $^1/_2$ (11.5 ounce) bag Ghirardelli Milk Chocolate Chips, $^1/_2$ (11.5 ounce) bag Ghirardelli 60% Cacao Bittersweet Chocolate Chips, or $^1/_2$ (11 ounce) bag Ghirardelli Classic White Chips
4 ounces unsweetened chocolate or baking chocolate	1 Ghirardelli 100% Cacao Unsweetened Chocolate baking bar
4 ounces semi-sweet chocolate	1 Ghirardelli Semi-Sweet Chocolate baking bar, 1 Ghirardelli 60% Cacao Bittersweet Chocolate baking bar, or 1 Ghirardelli 70% Cacao Extra Bittersweet baking bar

SAVORING CHOCOLATE WITH ALL YOUR SENSES

For a chocolate lover, the art of tasting—which is quite different from merely eating chocolate—has the power to transform a casual nibble into a world of new pleasures. The seemingly formal protocol used by professionals to compare and evaluate chocolates is simply a way of focusing attention on the chocolate, with all our senses. It's also loads of fun, challenging, and delicious!

Since no expertise or equipment is required, tasting can be done alone at home, with close friends after dinner, or you can make it a party full of fun and indulgence.

HOW TO TASTE AND APPRECIATE CHOCOLATE

The best chocolate is the one *you* like. In fact, no two people perceive aroma or taste flavors in exactly the same way. Even the perception of texture —whether something is smooth and creamy or slightly gritty—differs from one palate to another. Your individual chocolate palate also evolves and sharpens over time and with experience. Each taster should look for, notice, and describe what they like in each piece of chocolate.

To taste and appreciate chocolate, it is of utmost importance to engage all of your senses: sight, smell, touch, sound, and taste.

Appearance

We eat with our eyes. Appearance is part of the initial pleasure and attraction of chocolate, but it is not itself a measure of quality. The color of chocolate varies. It may be ivory, golden, shades of copper brown, deep reddish, or charcoal brown, depending on the type of chocolate, the percentage of cacao in the chocolate, the presence and quantity of milk and other ingredients, and the source of the beans from which the chocolate is made. An attractive gloss on the surface of chocolate with a tight, fine grain and even color showing at cut or broken edges indicates that the chocolate is well tempered and has been properly cooled and stored.

Aroma

As with wine, our nose gives us some of the first clues to flavor. Before even tasting, rub the piece of chocolate with your thumb to warm and release its aroma. Hold the chocolate to your nose in cupped hands to capture and hold the aroma close. Sniff or draw in slow breaths. At first chocolate may simply smell chocolaty. But as you compare one piece with another, you will notice general differences in the richness, intensity, sweetness, and earthiness. You'll pick up on lower notes and higher notes, distinctive flavors, or hints of flavor. The aroma of some chocolates is faint while in others it is intense. You may then detect even more specific differences.

Milk chocolates often give off aromas of milk or cream, or caramel or malt. Dark chocolate aromas may be characterized by toasted nuts, roasted coffee, dried fruit, or wine. Some chocolates have floral or fruity qualities; others smell more roasted or nutty. As with flavor, each chocolate brand has a signature aroma, which comes from the blend or selection of beans and their quality, as well as the manufacturer's roasting and conching methods. There is no end to the specific notes that you can pick up with practice and no limit to the words that you may use to describe them.

Texture

Texture is enormously important to the chocolate experience. A smooth and creamy melt-in-your-mouth texture can be so seductive that many people are more influenced by texture than by flavor.

Begin by listening for the snap! It is the first clue to texture. Snap is the feel and sound of a piece of chocolate when you first break it or bite into it. Snap is easier to appreciate in a thin bar than a thick chunk of chocolate. Snap is a function of the amount and quality of the cocoa butter in the chocolate, how finely ground the chocolate particles are, and how well the chocolate was tempered. A good chocolate snap should never be soft or crumbly.

White and milk chocolate bars have a gentler snap than dark or semi-sweet chocolate because their milk and butterfat content make them naturally softer.

Mouthfeel is another word for texture. After looking, smelling, and snapping, place the chocolate in your mouth. But resist the urge to chew and eat. Instead, hold the chocolate against the roof of your mouth and pass your tongue over the bottom of it, noticing first how it melts and then how it feels. Does it melt readily and feel smooth and creamy, or greasy and slimy? Maybe it resists melting and seems hard or waxy? Does it feel grainy or gritty, powdery, harsh, or drying?

No two palates have the same perception of these textures. It is even possible for the same piece of chocolate to seem smooth and silky to one taster and dry and powdery to the next.

Flavor

Flavor is the ultimate measure for quality in chocolate. Flavor begins to fill your mouth from the moment the chocolate begins to melt on your tongue.

At first there is so much pleasure in tasting the chocolate, it may be difficult to focus on the specifics of flavor. As with aroma, your first perception may be simply described as chocolaty. As you begin to focus, notice several things: Does the flavor come on quickly or slowly? Does the flavor build and peak or remain constant? Does the flavor change character from the beginning to the middle to the end? How long does the flavor last in your mouth? Professional chocolate tasters often look for a "long finish." This is simply flavor that lasts a long time in your mouth.

ENTERTAINING WITH CHOCOLATE

Looking for a new way to make that special party more memorable and special? Host a chocolate party! Theme your gathering entirely around chocolate. Offer your guests plenty of chocolate or chocolate desserts and spice it up with an exotic array of beverages and spirits for mixing and matching. Instead of serving the expected cocktails and nibbles, turn your next event into a "choc-tail party!" Or consider hosting a chocolate tasting party.

THE "CHOC-TAIL" PARTY

Feature an array of spectacular chocolate desserts featured in this book and attractive plates full of bite-size samples of delicious chocolate bars and squares. Top off the party by serving your favorite complementary beverages and chocolate food pairings. Pairing chocolate with wine and liquors is an elegant and sophisticated alternative to the usual cocktail party fare of cheese and crackers.

How to Stage It
Choose several complementary spirits and foods for your selected chocolates and recipes.

Choosing the Right Amount
If you are serving several chocolate desserts as well as several varieties of chocolate bars or squares at your "choc-tail party," plan on serving smaller amounts of each instead of full-size bars or servings. If you use Ghirardelli Squares™, plan on serving one square of each type of chocolate to each guest, and keep a dozen or so extras on hand. If you are featuring chocolate bars broken into smaller, one-inch, bite-size shards, plan on providing about two to three pieces of each type of chocolate per guest.

When planning how many of several different kinds of chocolate desserts you'll need, think in terms of serving one-quarter to one-third of a normal serving per guest. Provide plates large enough for tasting smaller servings of two or three chocolate desserts.

A fun touch is to create take-home party favors featuring a variety of chocolate samples for guests, or to provide guests with take-home party plates, which they can assemble as they leave.

HOSTING A CHOCOLATE TASTING

Bored with the usual wine and cheese parties? Be the first in your neighborhood or social circle to "wow" friends with a chocolate tasting party. Invite guests over to discover and practice tasting and appreciating chocolate together. You don't have to be an expert because all the knowledge and fun tools that you need are listed below. And everyone will discover something about chocolate they didn't know before!

How to Stage It

Consider how you'd like to theme your party—exclusively around exotic darks, creamy milk chocolates, or a tasty variety of darks, milks, and whites. As the party host, you'll want to brush up on how to taste chocolate on page 21. Plan your chocolate theme and go shopping for your chocolates. You will probably want to choose five to six different kinds of chocolate to sample.

Finally, consider your entertainment. Set the stage with elegant music. Consider lighting and romancing your chocolate table with candlelight.

Choosing the Chocolate

For a formal chocolate tasting party, plan to provide up to $1/2$ ounce of each type of chocolate (five to six kinds) per guest. (And keep an extra bar or two on hand, just in case.) Cut your bars into an assortment of sizes with the point of a sharp paring knife. Cut some into tiny bites and some into larger 1-inch shards as well (to allow tasters to bite into them). Try not to jumble or scuff the pieces, so that they remain visually enticing.

You may want to buy some extra bars for table display. And, consider buying extra bars for party favors. Give your guests a sample of each chocolate to take home and enjoy.

CHOCOLATE COOKIES

Ghirardelli Milk Chocolate Chip Cookies 28

Milk Chocolate Chip Cookies with Pecans 30

Oatmeal Chocolate Chip Cookies 31

Ultimate Double Chocolate Cookies 32

Peanut Butter Chocolate Cookies 34

Chocolate Mexican Wedding Cookies 35

Chocolate Checkerboards 37

Chocolate Shortbread Cookies 39

Double Chocolate Sugar Cookies 40

Chocolate-Dipped Lemon Cookies 41

Chocolate Gingerbread Men 42

Chocolate Apricot Rugelach 43

Black and White Macaroons 44

Double Chocolate–Hazelnut Biscotti 46

Marbled Biscotti 47

Dipping Chocolate for Biscotti 48

GHIRARDELLI MILK CHOCOLATE CHIP COOKIES

Makes 48 cookies

Preheat the oven to 375°F.

Stir together the flour, baking soda, and salt; set aside.

In a large bowl, beat the butter with the white and brown sugars using an electric mixer at medium speed until the mixture is creamy and lightened in color, about 4 minutes. Add the vanilla and eggs, one at a time, mixing on low speed until incorporated.

Gradually blend the flour mixture into the creamed mixture. Stir in the chocolate chips and nuts. Drop by the tablespoonful onto ungreased cookie sheets about 2 inches apart.

Bake for 9 to 11 minutes, until the cookies are golden brown. Transfer the cookies to wire racks to cool.

Store in airtight container at room temperature for up to one week.

VARIATION

CHOCOLATE CHIP COOKIES
Substitute Ghirardelli Semi-Sweet Chocolate Chips or 60% Cacao Bittersweet Chocolate Chips for the Milk Chocolate Chips.

2¼ cups all-purpose flour

1 teaspoon baking soda

½ teaspoon salt

1 cup (2 sticks) unsalted butter, at room temperature

1 cup granulated white sugar

1 cup firmly packed light or dark brown sugar

2 teaspoons pure vanilla extract

2 large eggs

2 cups Ghirardelli Milk Chocolate Chips

1 cup chopped walnuts or pecans (optional)

MILK CHOCOLATE CHIP COOKIES
WITH PECANS

Makes 48 cookies

Melt the bittersweet chocolate pieces in the top of a double boiler or in a heatproof bowl over barely simmering water, stirring occasionally until smooth.

In a large bowl, cream the butter, white sugar, and brown sugar with an electric mixer on medium-high speed until light and fluffy. Reduce the speed to low, and add the eggs and vanilla. Scrape the bottom and sides of the mixing bowl with a rubber spatula.

In a separate bowl, sift together the flour, baking powder, baking soda, salt, and espresso powder. Add half the flour mixture to the creamed butter, mixing well. Add half the melted chocolate and stir until ingredients are well blended. Add the remaining flour mixture, incorporating thoroughly, then add the remaining chocolate. Stir in the chocolate chips and pecans. Cover and refrigerate the dough for 1 hour.

Preheat the oven to 350°F. Line two cookie sheets with parchment paper.

Drop the dough in rounded tablespoonfuls onto the prepared cookie sheets, about 2 inches apart.

Bake for 15 to 17 minutes. Immediately slide the parchment paper and cookies onto a wire rack to cool. Store in an airtight container at room temperature for up to a week.

10 ounces Ghirardelli 60% Cacao Bittersweet Chocolate baking bars, broken or chopped into 1-inch pieces

½ cup (1 stick) unsalted butter, at room temperature

½ cup granulated white sugar

1 cup firmly packed light or dark brown sugar

4 large eggs

1 teaspoon pure vanilla extract

2¼ cups all-purpose flour

1 teaspoon baking powder

½ teaspoon baking soda

½ teaspoon salt

1 teaspoon powdered instant espresso (optional)

2 cups Ghirardelli Milk Chocolate Chips

1 cup pecans, coarsely chopped

OATMEAL CHOCOLATE CHIP COOKIES

Makes 60 cookies

Preheat the oven to 375°F.

In a large bowl, cream the butter with the brown and white sugars using an electric mixer at medium speed until creamy and lightened in color, about 4 minutes. Add the egg and vanilla, and mix on low speed until incorporated.

In a small bowl, stir together the flour, baking soda, salt, cinnamon, and nutmeg. Add to the creamed mixture, mixing well. Stir in the oats. Fold in the chocolate chips and walnuts. Drop by the rounded tablespoonful onto ungreased cookie sheets about 2 inches apart.

Bake 8 to 9 minutes for a chewy cookie, 10 to 11 minutes for a crisp cookie. Cool for 1 minute on the cookie sheets; remove to wire cooling racks.

Store in airtight container at room temperature for up to a week.

1 cup (2 sticks) butter, at room temperature

¾ cup firmly packed light or dark brown sugar

½ cup granulated white sugar

1 large egg

1 teaspoon pure vanilla extract

1 cup all-purpose flour

1 teaspoon baking soda

½ teaspoon salt

1 teaspoon ground cinnamon

⅛ teaspoon ground nutmeg

3 cups rolled oats

2 cups Ghirardelli Semi-Sweet Chocolate Chips

1 cup walnuts, chopped

ULTIMATE DOUBLE CHOCOLATE COOKIES

Makes 24 cookies

Melt the bittersweet chocolate chips and butter in the top of a double boiler or in a heatproof bowl over barely simmering water, stirring occasionally until smooth.

In a large bowl, beat the eggs and sugar with an electric mixer until thick; stir in the chocolate mixture. In a small bowl, stir together the flour and baking powder; stir into the chocolate mixture. Gently mix in the chocolate chips and walnuts.

Using a sheet of plastic wrap, form the dough into two logs, each 2 inches in diameter and about 8 inches long. Because the dough will be quite soft, use the plastic wrap to hold the dough in the log shape. Wrap tightly; refrigerate for at least 1 hour or until firm.

Preheat the oven to 375°F. Grease a cookie sheet or line with parchment paper.

Unwrap the dough. With a sharp knife, cut the dough into 3/4-inch slices. Place the slices 1 1/2 inches apart on the prepared cookie sheet.

Bake for 12 to 14 minutes, until a shiny crust forms on top of the cookies but the interior is still soft. Let cool on the cookie sheet. Then remove from the cookie sheet with a metal spatula.

Store in an airtight container at room temperature for up to one week.

2 cups Ghirardelli 60% Cacao Bittersweet Chocolate Chips

6 tablespoons (3/4 stick) unsalted butter

3 large eggs

1 cup granulated white sugar

1/3 cup all-purpose flour

1/2 teaspoon baking powder

2 cups Ghirardelli Semi-Sweet Chocolate Chips

1 cup chopped walnuts

PEANUT BUTTER CHOCOLATE COOKIES

Makes 48 cookies

Preheat the oven to 350°F.

In a large bowl, cream together the butter, peanut butter, brown sugar, and white sugar with an electric mixer until well blended. Beat in the egg, milk, and vanilla. In a separate bowl, stir together the flour, baking powder, and salt. Gradually add the dry ingredients to the creamed mixture. Stir in the chocolate chips and peanuts.

Drop by the teaspoonful onto an ungreased cookie sheet. Flatten with the tines of a fork to form a crisscross pattern.

Bake for 9 to 11 minutes, until the edges are golden brown. Allow to cool 1 minute on the cookie sheet, then transfer to a wire rack to cool completely. Store tightly covered at room temperature.

½ cup (1 stick) unsalted butter, at room temperature

½ cup creamy peanut butter

½ cup firmly packed light or dark brown sugar

¼ cup granulated white sugar

1 large egg

1 tablespoon whole milk

1 teaspoon pure vanilla extract

1 cup all-purpose flour

½ teaspoon baking powder

½ teaspoon salt

1 cup Ghirardelli Semi-Sweet Chocolate Chips

¾ cup dry-roasted unsalted peanuts, chopped

CHOCOLATE MEXICAN WEDDING COOKIES

Makes 16 cookies

To make the cookies, in a large bowl, cream the butter and confectioners' sugar with an electric mixer until light and fluffy. Add the vanilla.

In a separate bowl, stir together the flour, pecans, ground chocolate, cinnamon, and salt. Gradually add the dry ingredients to the creamed mixture and mix until well blended.

Wrap the dough in plastic wrap and chill for 1 to 2 hours, until firm.

Preheat the oven to 325°F.

Shape the dough into 1-inch balls. Place the balls 1 inch apart on an ungreased cookie sheet.

Bake for 15 to 18 minutes, until the cookies are firm to the touch. Cool for 1 minute on the cookie sheet, and then transfer to a wire rack.

To make the coating, sift the confectioners' sugar and ground chocolate into a shallow bowl. While the cookies are still warm, roll them in the coating.

Refrigerate airtight with waxed paper between layers up to 1 month.

Cookies

1 cup (2 sticks) unsalted butter, at room temperature

1/3 cup confectioners' sugar

2 teaspoons pure vanilla extract

1 3/4 cups all-purpose flour

1 cup ground pecans

1/2 cup Ghirardelli Sweet Ground Chocolate and Cocoa

3/4 teaspoon ground cinnamon

Pinch of salt

Coating

1/2 cup confectioners' sugar

1/4 cup Ghirardelli Sweet Ground Chocolate and Cocoa

CHOCOLATE CHECKERBOARDS

Makes 160 cookies

Sift together the flour, salt, and baking soda. Set aside.

Melt the bittersweet chocolate pieces in the top of a double boiler or in a heatproof bowl, over barely simmering water, stirring occasionally until smooth. Set aside.

In a large bowl, cream the butter with an electric mixer on medium-to-low speed until smooth, about 2 minutes. Mix in the sugar and beat for an additional 2 minutes. Add the egg and vanilla, mixing well until combined. Reduce the speed to low, and add the flour mixture in two additions, mixing until just incorporated. Separate out 2 cups of the dough and set aside.

Dissolve the espresso powder in the boiling water and set aside to cool. Once cool, mix the espresso and cocoa into the remaining dough until the dough is uniformly colored. On low speed, add in the melted chocolate, mixing until thoroughly combined.

Divide the dough into four equal pieces, two of each flavor. Shape each of the four pieces into a rectangular log 10 inches long, 3 inches wide, and ¾ inches thick. Wrap each log tightly in parchment paper and chill in the refrigerator for at least 30 minutes.

Cut each log into four quarters lengthwise, giving you 16 strips 10 inches long, ¾ inches wide, and ¾ inches thick. To form a checkerboard rectangle, place a chocolate strip and a vanilla strip side by side, and then place another vanilla strip on top of the chocolate strip and another chocolate strip on top of the vanilla strip. The checkerboard log should be about 10 inches long, 1½ inches wide, and 1½ inches thick. Repeat with the other 12 strips to make 3 more logs. Repeat until you have four checkerboard rectangles. Chill all the dough for at least 3 hours.

Preheat the oven to 350°F. Line two cookie sheets with parchment paper.

continued

3 cups all-purpose flour

½ teaspoon salt

¼ teaspoon baking soda

4 ounces Ghirardelli 60% Cacao Bittersweet Chocolate baking bar, broken or chopped into 1-inch pieces

1¼ cups (2½ sticks) unsalted butter, at room temperature

1¼ cups white granulated sugar

1 large egg

1½ teaspoons pure vanilla extract

1 teaspoon instant espresso powder

2 tablespoons boiling water

3 tablespoons Ghirardelli Unsweetened Cocoa

Make sure the dough is firm enough to slice, and use a sharp knife to slice each rectangle into ¼-inch squares and place 1 inch apart on the prepared baking sheet.

Bake for 12 to 13 minutes, making sure not to brown the edges too much. Remove the cookies from the oven, and let stand for 1 minute. Transfer to wire racks and let cool completely.

Store in an airtight container at room temperature for up to a week.

VARIATION

CHOCOLATE PINWHEEL COOKIES

Divide each flavor of dough (vanilla and chocolate) into three equal pieces. On pieces of plastic wrap, shape each piece of dough into a 5-inch by 5-inch square and wrap well. Note: The chocolate dough may be thicker than the vanilla. Chill the dough for at least 30 minutes in the refrigerator.

While the dough is chilling, tear off twelve 10-inch squares of parchment paper. Roll each piece of chilled dough into thinner 7-inch by 7-inch squares between two pieces of parchment paper. Without removing the parchment paper, layer the dough on a baking sheet and chill in the refrigerator for about 15 minutes. While chilling, tear three 13-inch sheets of plastic wrap.

To form the pinwheels, remove one square of the chocolate dough and one square of the vanilla dough from the refrigerator, peeling off the top sheet of paper from each. Invert the vanilla squares on top of the chocolate square (or vice versa, as desired). Trim the edges to make a neat square. Gently roll over the dough with a rolling pin to seal both doughs together. Peel off the top layer of parchment paper.

Starting with the edge of the dough nearest you and using your fingertips, slowly curl the edge of the bottom layer of dough up over the top layer, so there is no space in the center of the pinwheel. Continue rolling the dough tightly, jelly roll–style. Use the parchment paper to help you roll the dough into a cylinder.

After you form the cylinder, roll it gently back and forth on a flat surface to extend its length somewhat. Put the elongated cylinder on a cut piece of plastic wrap, and starting with the edge nearest you, roll it tightly and twist the ends of the plastic to seal. The dough should be between 8 and 9 inches long and 1½ inches thick. Refrigerate the dough cylinder, and repeat the above procedure with the remaining four pieces of dough. Allow the cylinders to chill for about 3 hours. Slice into ¼-inch rounds. Bake as above. Makes 96–108 cookies.

CHOCOLATE SHORTBREAD COOKIES

Makes 36 to 44 cookies

In a large bowl, cream the butter and sugar with an electric mixer on medium speed until smooth. Add the cocoa, flour, and salt. Mix on medium-low speed just until the dough comes together, about 1 minute. Refrigerate the dough for 30 minutes.

Preheat the oven to 325°F. Line two cookie sheets with parchment paper.

On a lightly floured board, roll out the dough to a thickness of 1/4 inch. Cut into 2-inch rounds. (Scraps can be rerolled.) Place the cookies on the prepared cookie sheets at least 1/2 inch apart. If the dough is very soft, refrigerate again for at least 30 minutes.

Bake for 15 minutes. Let cool on the cookie sheets, then remove with a metal spatula.

Store in airtight container for up to 5 days.

VARIATION

DIPPED CHOCOLATE SANDWICH COOKIES

Prepare the cookies as above. When cool, chop 4 ounces of the chocolate and melt in a double boiler or in a heatproof bowl over barely simmering water, stirring occasionally until smooth. Dip the tops of half of the cookies in the chocolate. (If the chocolate gets too thick and the cookies are too heavily coated, rewarm the chocolate slightly.) Set, chocolate-side up, on a parchment paper–lined baking sheet and leave until set, about 30 minutes.

Chop the remaining chocolate and melt in the top of a double boiler or in a heatproof bowl over barely simmering water. Remove from the heat and stir in the peanut butter until smooth. Let set until it has a spreading consistency, about 30 minutes. Spread about 2 teaspoons of the filling on the bottom of the undipped cookies. Place a dipped cookie, chocolate-side up, on top. Makes 22 sandwich cookies.

---

1 cup (2 sticks) unsalted butter, at room temperature

2/3 cup sugar

1/3 cup Ghirardelli Unsweetened Cocoa

2 cups all-purpose flour

1/4 teaspoon salt

8 ounces Ghirardelli Semi-Sweet Chocolate baking bar

1/2 cup smooth peanut butter

DOUBLE CHOCOLATE SUGAR COOKIES

Makes 24 cookies

To make the cookies, in a large bowl, cream the butter and sugar with an electric mixer at medium speed until light and fluffy. Beat in the egg and vanilla.

In a separate bowl, stir together the flour, ground chocolate, baking powder, and salt. Gradually add the dry ingredients to the creamed mixture, scraping down the sides of the bowl and the beaters with a rubber spatula as needed. Cover and chill the dough for 1 hour.

Preheat the oven to 325°F.

On a lightly floured surface, roll one-quarter of the dough to a thickness of ¼ inch. (Leave the remaining dough in the refrigerator until you are ready to use it.) With cookie cutters, cut the dough into desired shapes and place on ungreased cookie sheets, about 2 inches apart. Repeat with the remaining dough.

Bake for 5 to 7 minutes, until no indentation remains in a cookie when pressed lightly. Cool for 2 minutes on the cookie sheet, then transfer to wire racks to cool completely.

To make the glaze, melt the butter over low heat in a small, heavy saucepan. Remove from the heat and add the ground chocolate and 2 tablespoons of the water, whisking continually until the mixture is smooth. Add the vanilla. Gradually add the confectioners' sugar, stirring with a wire whisk until smooth. Add additional water, ½ teaspoon at a time, until the glaze reaches the desired consistency. Drizzle or spread on cooled cookies.

Cookies

½ cup (1 stick) unsalted butter, at room temperature

⅓ cup granulated white sugar

1 large egg

1 teaspoon pure vanilla extract

1½ cups all-purpose flour

⅔ cup Ghirardelli Sweet Ground Chocolate & Cocoa

½ teaspoon baking powder

¼ teaspoon salt

Glaze

2 tablespoons unsalted butter

½ cup Ghirardelli Sweet Ground Chocolate & Cocoa

2 to 3 tablespoons water

1½ teaspoons pure vanilla extract

¾ cup confectioners' sugar

CHOCOLATE-DIPPED LEMON COOKIES

Makes 60 cookies

In a large mixing bowl with an electric mixer on medium speed, cream the confectioners' sugar and butter until fluffy. Beat in the egg, lemon zest, lemon extract, and vanilla.

In a separate bowl, stir together the flour, baking powder, and salt. Add the dry ingredients to the wet ingredients, mixing just until combined. With well-floured hands, form the dough into a 1½-inch-wide log. Wrap the log in plastic wrap and refrigerate 30 to 60 minutes.

Preheat the oven to 350°F.

Slice the dough into ¼-inch-thick slices; place the rounds 1 inch apart on an ungreased cookie sheet.

Bake for 9 to 11 minutes, until edges are golden. Cool for 1 minute on the cookie sheet, and then transfer the cookies to a wire rack to cool completely.

To make the glaze, melt the chocolate in the top of a double boiler, or in a heatproof bowl, over barely simmering water, stirring occasionally until smooth. Add the melted butter and continue stirring until well blended.

Line two cookie sheets with parchment paper and coat lightly with nonstick cooking spray. Holding a cookie vertically, dip it halfway into the melted chocolate mixture. Place the cookie on one of the prepared cookie sheets. Repeat with the remaining cookies. Transfer the cookie sheets to a cool place and allow the chocolate to set, approximately 45 to 60 minutes. Store tightly covered at room temperature with parchment paper separating the layers.

Dough

1½ cups confectioners' sugar

1 cup (2 sticks) unsalted butter, at room temperature

1 large egg

2 teaspoons grated lemon zest

1 teaspoon lemon extract

1 teaspoon pure vanilla extract

2½ cups all-purpose flour

1 teaspoon baking powder

¼ teaspoon salt

Glaze

12 ounces Ghirardelli Semi-Sweet Chocolate baking bars, broken or chopped into 1-inch pieces

1½ tablespoons unsalted butter, melted

CHOCOLATE GINGERBREAD MEN

Makes 40 cookies

These also make fun sandwich cookies. For a nice contrast, use the White Chocolate Frosting recipe (see page 70) to create a filling between two gingerbread men. Use frosting to decorate as desired.

Melt the chocolate in the top of a double boiler or in a heatproof bowl over simmering water, stirring occasionally until smooth. Set aside to cool.

In a large bowl, sift together the flour, cocoa, baking soda, and salt. Set aside.

In an large bowl with an electric mixer on medium speed, beat the butter, brown sugar, white sugar, ginger, cinnamon, cloves, and nutmeg until the mixture is light and fluffy, about 2 minutes. Add the molasses, egg, and melted chocolate and continue beating on medium speed for an additional 2 minutes. On low speed, slowly add the dry ingredients and mix just until combined.

Transfer the dough to a flat surface and flatten into a disk. Cover with plastic wrap and chill in the refrigerator for at least 1 hour, or up to 5 days.

Preheat the oven to 350°F. Line two cookie sheets with parchment paper.

Divide the chilled dough into four equal quarters, leaving three quarters in the refrigerator. Lightly flour a flat work surface and roll out one piece of dough to a thickness of about $1/8$ inch. Using a small (2 to $2\frac{1}{2}$-inch) gingerbread man or -woman cookie cutter, cut out as many cookies as possible. Place the cookies on the prepared cookie sheets, about 1 inch apart. Gather all the dough scraps into a ball and place in the refrigerator. Take out another quarter of the dough, and continue rolling out the dough and cutting cookies until all the dough has been used.

Bake the cookies for 8 to 10 minutes until slightly raised. Using a spatula, remove the cookies from the cookie sheets, transferring to a wire rack to cool.

4 ounces Ghirardelli 60% Cacao Bittersweet Chocolate baking bar, broken or chopped into 1-inch pieces

3 cups all-purpose flour

$1/2$ cup Ghirardelli Unsweetened Cocoa

1 teaspoon baking soda

$1/4$ teaspoon salt

$3/4$ cup ($1\frac{1}{2}$ sticks) unsalted butter, at room temperature

$1/2$ cup firmly packed dark brown sugar

$1/2$ cup granulated white sugar

2 tablespoons ground ginger

2 teaspoons ground cinnamon

$1/2$ teaspoon ground cloves

$1/4$ teaspoon ground nutmeg

$1/4$ cup molasses

1 large egg

CHOCOLATE APRICOT RUGELACH

Makes 48 cookies

These cookies are filled with spreadable fruit, which can be found in the jam aisle. We found Smuckers to work best because it is not too sweet.

To make the dough, combine the flour and confectioners' sugar in a food processor and process to blend. Add the butter and cream cheese and process until the dough forms a ball.

Divide the dough into four equal portions. With floured hands, pat each portion into a 1/2-inch thick disk. Lightly flour the surface of each. Place each portion between two (12-inch by 15-inch) pieces of floured plastic wrap, placing the floured side against the dough. Roll each portion into a 9-inch circle about 1/8-inch thick. Stack the wrapped rounds on a baking sheet and chill for 30 minutes, or up to 1 day, until the dough is firm to the touch.

Heat the oven to 350°F. Line cookie sheets with parchment paper.

To make the toppings, in a small bowl, beat together the egg and milk. In another small bowl, mix the granulated white sugar and cinnamon.

To fill the dough, work with one dough round at a time, keeping the remaining rounds chilled. With a floured knife, cut the round into 12 equal wedges and leave the pieces in place. Smear 2 tablespoons of the apricot spread all over the dough round. Sprinkle 5 tablespoons chocolate and 1 tablespoon nuts evenly over the apricot spread; press lightly into the dough. Starting at wide end of each wedge, roll up tightly and set on parchment-lined cookie sheet, tail-end down. Place the cookies at least 2 inches apart. Repeat to fill the remaining dough. Brush each with egg-milk mixture and sprinkle with the cinnamon sugar.

Bake for 20 to 25 minutes, until golden. If you are baking two sheets at a time in one oven, switch the sheet positions halfway through baking.

Let the cookies cool on the sheets for about 5 minutes. Run a thin spatula underneath each cookie to release it from the parchment paper. Finish cooling on the sheets. Store in an airtight container for up to 1 week.

Dough

2 cups all-purpose flour

1/2 cup confectioners' sugar

1 cup (2 sticks) unsalted butter, cut into 1/2-inch pieces

8 ounces cream cheese, cut into 1/2-inch pieces

Toppings

1 large egg

1 tablespoon whole milk

1/4 cup granulated white sugar

1 teaspoon ground cinnamon

Filling

1/2 cup apricot spreadable fruit

6 ounces Ghirardelli Semi-Sweet or Milk Chocolate baking bars, finely chopped

1/4 cup finely chopped walnuts or pecans

BLACK AND WHITE MACAROONS

Makes 48 cookies

Preheat the oven to 300°F. Line two baking sheets with aluminum foil.

In a large bowl, beat the egg whites with an electric mixer until foamy. Add the cream of tartar and salt; continue beating until soft peaks form. Gradually add the sugar and vanilla, beating until stiff but not dry. Fold in the coconut and 1 cup of the chocolate chips.

Drop by rounded teaspoonfuls onto the prepared baking sheets, 1 to 2 inches apart. Sprinkle the cookies with the remaining 1/2 cup of chocolate chips.

Bake for 20 minutes, or until the surfaces begin to crack. Cool completely before removing the cookies from the foil. Store loosely covered at room temperature.

Note: Humidity has an adverse effect on meringues. For best results, make this recipe on a day with low humidity.

3 large egg whites

1/4 teaspoon cream of tartar

1/4 teaspoon salt

1 cup granulated white sugar

1 teaspoon pure vanilla extract

2 cups flaked coconut

1 1/2 cups Ghirardelli Semi-Sweet Chocolate Chips

DOUBLE CHOCOLATE–HAZELNUT BISCOTTI

Makes 48 cookies

These biscotti are also nice with almonds in place of the hazelnuts, or a mix of both. For an even more chocolatey version, dip the biscotti in melted chocolate (see page 48.)

Preheat the oven to 350°. Lightly grease two cookie sheets.

In a large bowl, whisk together the flour, sugar, baking powder, salt, baking soda, ground chocolate, and semi-sweet chocolate.

In a separate bowl, combine the eggs and vanilla, and stir until well blended. Pour the egg mixture into the dry ingredients. Beat with an electric mixer on medium speed until a dough forms (it should adhere to the beaters), 2 to 3 minutes. Fold in the nuts.

Divide the dough into four equal parts. On the prepared cookie sheets, using lightly floured hands, shape each portion into 1¼-inch by 10-inch logs. Place the logs at least 4 inches apart.

Bake for 25 to 30 minutes, until the logs are firm to the touch.

Let cool on the cookie sheets for 15 minutes, or until cool enough to handle.

Lower the oven temperature to 300°F.

Transfer one log to a cutting board and, with a serrated knife, cut into twelve 1-inch-wide cookies. Repeat with the remaining three logs. Remove one oven rack and place the 48 cookies directly on it. Return the rack to the uppermost position in the oven and bake for 20 to 25 minutes, until crisp. To test for doneness, remove one cookie; let it cool, then check for crispness.

Transfer the cookies from the oven rack to a wire cooling rack and let cool completely. Store at room temperature in a tightly covered container.

2 cups all-purpose flour

1 cup granulated white sugar

2½ teaspoons baking powder

½ teaspoon salt

½ teaspoon baking soda

½ cup Ghirardelli Sweet Ground Chocolate & Cocoa

4 ounces Ghirardelli Semi-Sweet Chocolate baking bar, finely chopped

3 large eggs

1 teaspoon pure vanilla extract

1 cup hazelnuts, coarsely chopped

MARBLED BISCOTTI

Makes 48 cookies

Preheat the oven to 350°F. Lightly grease two cookie sheets.

Melt the chocolate chips in the top of a double boiler or in a heatproof bowl over barely simmering water, stirring occasionally until smooth. Remove from the heat and cool.

In a large bowl, beat the butter with an electric mixer on medium speed until it is creamy, about 1 minute. Add the sugar, baking powder, and salt; beat until blended. Beat in the eggs and vanilla until combined. Stir in the flour with a wooden spoon.

Divide the dough in half and transfer one half to another bowl. Stir the melted chocolate and 1/4 cup of the hazelnuts into one-half of the dough. Stir the orange zest and remaining nuts into the other half. Divide each half into four equal parts. Using lightly floured hands, shape each portion into a 1 1/4-inch by 10-inch rope. Place a rope of each color side by side on one of the prepared baking sheets. Twist the ropes around each other several times. Flatten slightly to make a 2-inch-wide log. Repeat with the other ropes, placing the resulting logs about 4 inches apart on the baking sheets.

Bake for 25 minutes, or until the logs are firm to the touch. Cool on the baking sheets for 15 minutes, or until cool enough to handle. Lower the oven temperature to 300°F.

Transfer one log to a cutting board and, with a serrated knife, cut the log into twelve 1-inch-wide cookies. Repeat with the remaining three logs. Remove one oven rack and place the 48 cookies directly on it. Return the rack to the uppermost position in the oven and bake for 20 to 25 minutes, until crisp. To test for doneness, remove one cookie; let it cool, then check it for crispness.

Transfer the cookies from the oven rack to a wire cooling rack and let cool completely. Store at room temperature in a tightly covered container.

3/4 cup Ghirardelli Semi-Sweet Chocolate Chips

1/3 cup (2/3 stick) unsalted butter, at room temperature

3/4 cup granulated white sugar

2 teaspoons baking powder

Pinch of salt

2 large eggs

1/2 teaspoon pure vanilla extract

2 cups all-purpose flour

1/2 cup hazelnuts, coarsely chopped

1 1/2 teaspoons grated orange zest

DIPPING CHOCOLATE FOR BISCOTTI

Makes 1½ cups

Line two baking sheets with parchment paper.

Melt the chocolate and the shortening in the top of a double boiler or in a heatproof bowl over barely simmering water, stirring occasionally until smooth. Remove the dip from the heat.

Holding a cookie horizontally, dip one side of the biscotti into the mixture to cover the side and half of the top and bottom portions of the cookie. Place the biscotti, chocolate-dipped side down, on one of the prepared baking sheets. Repeat with the remaining biscotti. Transfer the baking sheets to a cool place and allow the chocolate to set, 45 to 60 minutes.

1½ cups Ghirardelli Semi-Sweet Chocolate Chips

2 tablespoons solid vegetable shortening

CHOCOLATE BROWNIES
AND BARS

Classic Chocolate Brownies. 52

Fudgy Chocolate Brownies 53

Peppermint Brownies 54

Chocolate Caramel Brownies. 56

Classic Blondies. 57

Cherry and White Chocolate Brownies. 59

Chocolate and Peanut Butter Cheesecake Bars 60

CLASSIC CHOCOLATE BROWNIES

Makes 16 brownies

Preheat the oven to 350°F. Butter and flour an 8-inch square baking pan.

In the top of a double boiler or in a heatproof bowl over barely simmering water, melt the chocolate and butter, stirring occasionally until smooth. Remove the pan from the heat and let cool to room temperature.

Stir the brown sugar and vanilla into the chocolate mixture. Add the eggs and mix well.

In a bowl, sift together flour, baking powder, and salt. Slowly fold the flour mixture into the chocolate mixture, mixing well until blended. Stir in the chocolate chips and pour the batter into the prepared pan.

Bake for 25 to 30 minutes, until a tester comes out clean. Remove from the oven and cool for at least 10 minutes before cutting into 2-inch squares.

4 ounces Ghirardelli Semi-Sweet Chocolate baking bar, broken or chopped into 1-inch pieces

½ cup (1 stick) unsalted butter, cut into pieces

1 cup firmly packed light or dark brown sugar

1 teaspoon pure vanilla extract

2 large eggs

¾ cup plus 2 tablespoons all-purpose flour

¼ teaspoon baking powder

½ teaspoon salt

½ cup Ghirardelli Semi-Sweet Chocolate Chips

FUDGY CHOCOLATE BROWNIES

Makes 16 brownies

Preheat the oven to 325°F. Butter an 8-inch square baking pan and line it with parchment paper, buttered on both sides.

Melt the chocolate and butter in the top of a double boiler or a heatproof bowl over barely simmering water, stirring occasionally until smooth. Remove from the heat.

Using a large spoon, beat the sugar and salt into the chocolate mixture. Then beat in the eggs, one at a time. Add the flour and mix until the batter pulls away from the sides of the bowl. Pour the batter into the prepared pan.

Bake for 30 to 35 minutes, until a tester inserted into the center comes out clean.

Remove from oven and cool for at least 10 minutes. Remove the brownies from the pan, and let cool completely before cutting into 2-inch squares.

8 ounces Ghirardelli 60% Cacao Bittersweet Chocolate baking bar, broken or chopped into 1-inch pieces

6 tablespoons (¾ stick) unsalted butter, cut into pieces

¾ cup granulated white sugar

Pinch of salt

2 large eggs

⅓ cup all-purpose flour

PEPPERMINT BROWNIES

Makes 16 brownies

To serve these at a party, or to package them nicely to give away for the holiday season, cut the brownies smaller and place them in paper candy cups.

Preheat the oven to 350°F. Spray a 9-inch square baking pan with cooking spray and dust with flour, tapping out any excess.

In the top of a double boiler or in a heatproof bowl over barely simmering water, melt the unsweetened chocolate and butter, stirring occasionally until smooth. Cool to room temperature.

In a large bowl with an electric mixer or whisk, beat the eggs, sugar, vanilla, peppermint extract, and salt until combined. Beat in the chocolate mixture. Gently stir in the flour. Pour the batter into the prepared pan.

Bake for about 45 minutes, or until a tester inserted into the brownies comes out clean. Arrange the mint squares on top in one layer and return the brownies to the oven until they are just melted, about 1 minute. Evenly spread the chocolate with a spatula and sprinkle with the crushed candy canes. Cool completely before cutting into 2-inch squares.

4 ounces Ghirardelli 100% Cacao Unsweetened Chocolate baking bar, broken or chopped into 1-inch pieces

1 cup (2 sticks) unsalted butter

3 large eggs

2 cups granulated white sugar

1 teaspoon pure vanilla extract

1/2 teaspoon peppermint extract

1/4 teaspoon salt

1 cup all-purpose flour

1 (5.32-ounce) bag Ghirardelli Dark Chocolate with White Mint Filling Squares™ (about 10 squares), unwrapped

4 small candy canes, crushed (about 1/4 cup)

CHOCOLATE CARAMEL BROWNIES

Makes 16 brownies

Preheat the oven to 350°F. Butter an 8-inch square baking pan.

In a medium bowl, beat the eggs with the sugar and vanilla. Add the melted butter and mix well.

In another bowl, sift together the ground chocolate, flour, baking powder, and salt. Stir into the egg mixture.

Spread half the batter in the prepared pan. Place the chocolate squares in a single layer on top of the batter to cover completely, then cover with the remaining batter.

Bake for 20 to 30 minutes, until a tester inserted in the center comes out clean. Cool completely before cutting into 2-inch squares.

2 large eggs

¼ cup granulated white sugar

1 teaspoon pure vanilla extract

½ cup (1 stick) unsalted butter, melted

1¼ cups Ghirardelli Sweet Ground Chocolate & Cocoa

⅔ cup all-purpose flour

¼ teaspoon baking powder

¼ teaspoon salt

12 to 16 Ghirardelli Milk Chocolate with Caramel Filling Squares™, unwrapped

CLASSIC BLONDIES

Makes 16 bars

Preheat the oven to 350°F. Line a 9-inch square baking pan with parchment paper. Grease the paper.

In the top of a double boiler or in a heatproof bowl over barely simmering water, melt the white chocolate and butter, stirring occasionally until smooth.

In a large bowl with an electric mixer at medium speed, beat the eggs until foamy. With the mixer running, add the sugar in a slow, steady stream. Add the vanilla. Add the melted chocolate and butter in a thin stream. With a rubber spatula, fold in the flour, salt, and chocolate chips until well combined. Spoon the mixture into the prepared pan.

Bake for 25 minutes, or until a tester comes out clean when inserted into the center. Let the brownies cool for at least 10 minutes. Cut and serve warm or at room temperature. Store in an airtight container at room temperature.

8 ounces Ghirardelli White Chocolate baking bar, broken or chopped into 1-inch pieces

1/2 cup (1 stick) unsalted butter, cut into small pieces

2 large eggs

1/3 cup granulated white sugar

1 tablespoon pure vanilla extract

1 1/4 cups all-purpose flour

3/4 teaspoon salt

1 cup Ghirardelli Semi-Sweet Chocolate Chips or Milk Chocolate Chips

CHERRY AND WHITE CHOCOLATE BROWNIES

Makes 16 brownies

These dark, fudgy brownies can stand alone, but for an indulgent plated dessert, top them with slightly sweetened softly whipped cream and a dusting of cocoa.

Preheat the oven to 325°F. Butter an 8-inch square baking pan. Line the bottom and two sides of the pan with a piece of parchment paper; press the parchment paper smoothly against the pan—excess can extend over pan rim.

In a small pan over low heat, cook the cherries and kirsch just until liquid begins to bubble, about 1 minute. Remove from the heat and let stand for 5 to 10 minutes, until the cherries absorb most of the liquid.

In the top of a double boiler or in a heatproof bowl over barely simmering water, melt the bittersweet chocolate and butter, stirring occasionally until smooth. Remove from the heat.

With a wooden spoon, beat the eggs, sugar, and salt in a medium bowl until blended. Stir in the melted chocolate mixture. Add the flour, stirring until blended. Stir the white chocolate pieces and cherry mixture into the batter. Spread the batter in the prepared pan.

Bake for 35 to 38 minutes, until a thin shiny crust forms on top and the center is soft when gently pressed.

Cool completely in the pan on a rack for at least 1½ hours. Cut around the pan sides where there is no parchment paper. Lift the brownie out of the pan, then cut it into squares, wiping the blade clean after each cut.

½ cup dried cherries

2 tablespoons kirsch

6 ounces Ghirardelli 60% Cacao Bittersweet Chocolate baking bar, broken or chopped into ½-inch pieces

½ cup (1 stick) unsalted butter, cut into ½-inch pieces

3 large eggs

¾ cup granulated white sugar

¼ teaspoon salt

¾ cup all-purpose flour

4 ounces Ghirardelli White Chocolate baking bar, broken or chopped into ½-inch pieces

CHOCOLATE AND PEANUT BUTTER CHEESECAKE BARS

Makes 24 bars

Preheat the oven to 350°F.

To make the crust, combine the crushed graham crackers, ground chocolate, butter, and sugar in a large bowl until well blended. Press the mixture onto the bottom of an ungreased 9 by 13-inch baking pan. Bake for 8 minutes, and then transfer to a wire rack and let cool.

While the crust cools, make the cheesecake layer. In a large bowl, beat the cream cheese, sugar, peanut butter, and flour with an electric mixer at low speed until well blended. Add the eggs, one at a time, mixing well after each addition. Mix in the milk and vanilla. Pour the filling into the crust.

Bake for 40 minutes, or until just set. Place the pan on a wire rack and let cool completely.

Melt the milk chocolate and vegetable shortening in the top of a double boiler, or in a heatproof bowl, over barely simmering water, stirring occasionally until smooth. Spread the melted chocolate evenly over the cooled bars. Chill for approximately 10 minutes, just until the chocolate layer is partially set. Score the chocolate layer with a sharp knife, forming 2-inch squares (approximately), and return the pan to the refrigerator. Chill for 30 minutes, or until firm. Cut through the bars and serve. Store tightly covered in the refrigerator.

Crust

2 cups crushed graham crackers

1/2 cup Ghirardelli Sweet Ground Chocolate & Cocoa

1/2 cup (1 stick) butter, melted

2 tablespoons granulated white sugar

Cheesecake Layer

16 ounces cream cheese, at room temperature

1 cup granulated white sugar

1/2 cup creamy peanut butter

3 tablespoons all-purpose flour

4 large eggs

1/2 cup whole milk

1 teaspoon pure vanilla extract

2 ounces Ghirardelli Milk Chocolate baking bar, broken or chopped into 1-inch pieces

1/2 teaspoon solid vegetable shortening

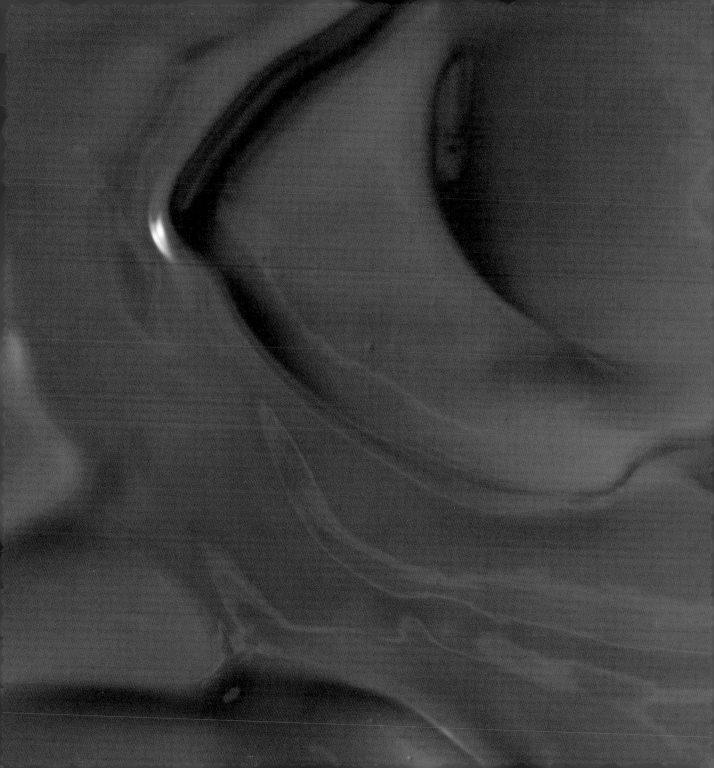

CHOCOLATE CAKES, CUPCAKES, AND TORTES

Devil's Food Cake with Sinful Chocolate Frosting 64

German Chocolate Cake 66

White Chocolate Peppermint Cake 67

Dark Chocolate Cupcakes 68

White Chocolate Cupcakes 70

Cinnamon-Scented Chocolate Angel Food Cake 71

Flourless Chocolate Torte with Dark Chocolate Glaze 73

Triple Chocolate Truffle Cake 75

Individual Soft Center Cakes 76

Flourless Mocha Torte 78

Chocolate Caramel Walnut Torte 80

Passover Dark Chocolate Velvet Torte 81

Chocolate-Almond Layered Cheesecake 82

Chocolate Chip Cheesecake 85

Chocolate Orange Cheesecake 86

DEVIL'S FOOD CAKE WITH SINFUL CHOCOLATE FROSTING

Makes 12 to 16 servings

If you like a very tall layer cake, double all of the ingredients for four layers instead of two.

Preheat the oven to 325°F. Butter the bottoms and sides of two 9 by 2-inch round cake pans, and line with parchment paper.

To make the cake, in the top of a double boiler or in a heatproof bowl over barely simmering water, melt together the bittersweet chocolate, butter, sugar, and corn syrup, stirring occasionally until smooth. Remove from the heat and set aside.

In a medium bowl, sift together the flour, cocoa, and baking soda. Gently mix in the melted chocolate mixture. Add in the eggs, vanilla, and milk and beat with a spoon until well blended. Divide the mixture evenly between the two prepared pans.

Bake for 25 to 29 minutes, until firm to the touch. Remove from the oven and cool on wire racks. When cool, turn out of the pans.

While the cake is cooling, make the frosting. In the top of a double boiler, or in a heatproof bowl over barely simmering water, melt the bittersweet and milk chocolates, stirring occasionally until smooth. Remove from the heat. Beat in the sour cream.

Spread one-third of the frosting on top of one cake layer, then set the second layer on top. Use the remaining frosting to spread over the top and sides of the cake. Let sit in a cool spot, but do not chill in the refrigerator. This cake is best if enjoyed within 4 days of baking.

Cake

4 ounces Ghirardelli 60% Cacao Bittersweet Chocolate baking bar, broken or chopped into 1-inch pieces

1/2 cup (1 stick) unsalted butter

1/2 cup firmly packed light or dark brown sugar

1 tablespoon light corn syrup

1 cup all-purpose flour

1/4 cup Ghirardelli Unsweetened Cocoa

1/2 teaspoon baking soda

2 large eggs, beaten

1/2 teaspoon pure vanilla extract

1/2 cup whole milk

Chocolate Frosting

6 ounces Ghirardelli 60% Cacao Bittersweet Chocolate baking bar, broken or chopped into 1-inch pieces

6 ounces Ghirardelli Milk Chocolate Baking bar, broken or chopped into 1-inch pieces

1 cup sour cream

GERMAN CHOCOLATE CAKE

Makes 12 to 16 servings

Preheat the oven to 350°F. Line three 8-inch or 9-inch round cake pans with parchment paper.

In the top of a double boiler or in a heatproof bowl over barely simmering water, melt the chocolate with the water, stirring until smooth.

In a large bowl, cream the butter with the sugar using an electric mixer until light and fluffy. Add the egg yolks, one at a time, beating after each addition. Mix in the melted chocolate and vanilla.

Sift the flour with the baking soda. Add the dry ingredients alternately with the buttermilk to chocolate mixture. Mix until smooth.

Beat the egg whites with the salt until very stiff peaks form. Fold into the batter.

Spread into the prepared cake pans.

Bake for 30 to 35 minutes. Cool on a wire rack for 10 minutes; remove the cakes from the pans. Cool completely and peel off the parchment paper before frosting.

To make the frosting, in a heavy saucepan over medium heat, melt the butter completely. Add the half-and-half, brown sugar, and egg yolks, blending with a whisk until the mixture begins to boil. Reduce to low heat and continue to stir for 5 to 7 minutes, until the frosting has thickened. Add the vanilla, then fold in the pecans and coconut.

To assemble the cake, spread some of the frosting over the top of one of the cake layers. Place a second cake layer on top and frost and repeat with the third cake layer. Frost the sides of the cake.

Cake

4 ounces Ghirardelli Semi-Sweet Chocolate baking bar, broken or chopped into 1-inch pieces

1/2 cup water

1 cup (2 sticks) unsalted butter, at room temperature

2 cups granulated white sugar

4 large eggs, separated

1 teaspoon pure vanilla extract

2 cups all-purpose flour, sifted

1 teaspoon baking soda

1 cup buttermilk

1/2 teaspoon salt

Butter Pecan Frosting

1/2 cup (1 stick) butter

1 cup half-and-half

1 cup firmly packed light or dark brown sugar

3 large egg yolks

1 teaspoon pure vanilla extract

1 cup pecans, chopped

1 cup flaked coconut

WHITE CHOCOLATE PEPPERMINT CAKE

Makes 8 to 12 servings

Preheat the oven to 350°F. Grease the bottom and sides of two 9-inch round cake pans and line the bottoms with parchment paper.

Sift together the flour, baking powder, and salt. In a large bowl with an electric mixer on medium speed, cream the butter with the sugar. Add the eggs scraping down the sides of the bowl between each addition. In a small bowl, stir together the milk, lemon juice, and the vanilla extract. On low speed, add half the milk. Mix until combined. Add half the dry ingredients. Mix until combined and scrape down the sides of the bowl. Add the remaining milk and the dry ingredients in the same manner. Divide the batter between the two pans.

Bake on the center oven rack for 15 minutes, until a tester inserted comes out clean. Allow to cool for 10 minutes, then unmold the cakes on a rack. Cool completely. Peel off the parchment paper.

To make the frosting, melt the white chocolate in the top of a double boiler, or in a heatproof bowl, over barely simmering water, stirring occasionally until smooth. Cool to room temperature.

While the chocolate is cooling, combine the egg whites and sugar in the bowl of an electric mixer. Place the bowl in a pot of simmering water so the water comes a third of the way up the bowl. Lightly whisk the egg whites just until warm to the touch, about 1½ minutes. Remove the bowl from the pot and mix on high speed until very thick and cooled to room temperature, about 5 minutes. Decrease to medium-low and add the butter, 1 tablespoon at a time. Add the white chocolate and vanilla and mix until smooth. Let sit for 5 minutes. Crush the peppermint candies into small pieces. Sift the crushed candies and discard any peppermint dust.

To assemble the cake, spread about 1¼ cups of the frosting over the top of one of the cake layers. Place the second layer on top and frost the top and sides of the cake. To get the crushed candy onto the sides of the cake, keep your hand about 1 inch from the sides of the cake and gently toss the candy onto the frosting.

Cake

1¾ cups plus 2 tablespoons all-purpose flour

¾ teaspoon baking powder

¼ teaspoon salt

¾ cup (1½ sticks) unsalted butter, at room temperature

1½ cups granulated white sugar

3 large eggs

¾ cup milk

¾ teaspoon fresh lemon juice

1½ teaspoons pure vanilla extract

White Chocolate Frosting

6 ounces Ghirardelli White Chocolate baking bar, broken or chopped into 1-inch pieces

4 large egg whites

1 cup plus 2 tablespoons sugar

1 cup plus 2 tablespoons (2¼ sticks) unsalted butter, at room temperature

1½ teaspoons pure vanilla extract

8 ounces (about 45) round peppermint candies

DARK CHOCOLATE CUPCAKES

Makes 12 cupcakes

Preheat the oven to 350°F. Line 12 cupcake molds or muffin tins with paper liners or spray with nonstick spray.

To make the cupcakes, sift together the flour, cocoa, baking soda, and salt.

In a medium bowl, whisk together the egg, brown sugar, and white sugar. Whisk in the milk, coffee, and melted butter. Whisk in the dry ingredients. Divide the batter evenly among the cupcake molds, filling them about three-quarters full.

Bake for 15 minutes, or until a tester inserted in the middle of the cupcakes comes out clean. Cool for 10 minutes. Using a small spatula or knife, remove the cupcakes from the pan. Continue to cool on a wire rack to room temperature.

To make the frosting, melt the chopped chocolate in the top of a double boiler or in a heatproof bowl over barely simmering water, stirring occasionally until smooth. Heat the cream until hot. Remove from the heat and whisk in the chocolate. Transfer to a bowl and cool to just warm. Whisk in the butter until smooth. Let sit until it reaches a spreading consistency, about 1 hour. Spread the frosting on top of the cupcakes. Sprinkle them with the chocolate chips.

Cupcakes

1 cup plus 2 tablespoons all-purpose flour

¼ cup Ghirardelli Unsweetened Cocoa

1¼ teaspoons baking soda

¼ teaspoon salt

1 large egg

½ cup firmly packed light brown sugar

½ cup granulated white sugar

½ cup plus 2 tablespoons whole milk

⅓ cup strong brewed coffee or espresso

½ cup (1 stick) unsalted butter, melted

Frosting

6 ounces Ghirardelli Semi-Sweet Chocolate baking bar, broken or chopped into 1-inch pieces, or 1 cup Ghirardelli Semi-Sweet Chocolate Chips

¾ cup heavy cream

3 tablespoons unsalted butter

1 cup Ghirardelli Milk Chocolate or Semi-Sweet Chocolate Chips for garnish

Dark Chocolate Cupcake (left) and
White Chocolate Cupcake (right, page 70)

WHITE CHOCOLATE CUPCAKES

Makes 14 cupcakes

Pictured on page 69

Preheat the oven to 350°F. Line 14 cupcake molds or muffin tins with paper liners or spray with nonstick spray.

Sift together the flour, baking powder, and salt.

To make the cupcakes, in a large bowl, beat the butter and sugar with an electric mixer on medium speed until light. Add the eggs, one at a time, scraping down the sides of the bowl between each addition. Stir together the milk, lemon juice, and the vanilla. On low speed, add half the milk mixture. Mix until incorporated; scrape down the sides of the bowl. Add half the dry ingredients. Mix until combined and scrape down the sides of the bowl. Add the remaining milk mixture and the dry ingredients in the same manner. Divide the batter among the 14 cupcake molds.

Bake on the middle oven rack for about 15 minutes, or until a tester inserted in the center of the cupcakes comes out clean. Cool cupcakes in their pans for 10 minutes. Then unmold and cool on a wire rack.

To make the frosting, melt the white chocolate in the top of a double boiler, or in a heatproof bowl over barely simmering water, stirring occasionally until smooth. Cool to room temperature.

While the chocolate is cooling, combine the egg whites and sugar in the bowl of an electric mixer. Place the bowl in a pot of simmering water so the water comes a third of the way up the bowl. Lightly whisk the egg whites just until hot to the touch, about 1½ minutes. Remove the bowl from the pot and whisk on high speed until very thick and cooled to room temperature, about 5 minutes. Decrease the mixer to medium-low speed and add the butter, 1 tablespoon at a time, mixing the butter in before adding the next tablespoon. Add the white chocolate and vanilla and mix until smooth.

Frost the top of each cupcake and sprinkle them with the white chocolate chips.

Cupcakes

1¾ cups plus 2 tablespoons all-purpose flour

¾ teaspoon baking powder

¼ teaspoon salt

¾ cup (1½ sticks) unsalted butter, at room temperature

1½ cups granulated white sugar

3 large eggs

¾ cup whole milk

¾ teaspoon fresh lemon juice

1½ teaspoons pure vanilla extract

White Chocolate Frosting

6 ounces Ghirardelli White Chocolate baking bar, chopped or broken into 1-inch pieces

4 large egg whites

1 cup plus 2 tablespoons granulated white sugar

1 cup plus 2 tablespoons (2¼ sticks) unsalted butter, at room temperature

1½ teaspoons pure vanilla extract

1 cup Ghirardelli Classic White Chocolate Chips for garnish

CINNAMON-SCENTED CHOCOLATE ANGEL FOOD CAKE

Makes 12 to 16 servings

In this recipe, the angel food cake is topped with a chocolate glaze. If you prefer, this cake also can be served plain or dusted with confectioners' sugar or cocoa.

Preheat the oven to 350°F. Set out a 10 by 4-inch tube pan with a removable bottom but do not grease.

To make the cake, sift the cake flour, confectioners' sugar, cocoa, and cinnamon into a bowl. Whisk lightly to blend.

In a large bowl with an electric mixer on high speed, whip the egg whites, cream of tartar, and salt until foamy. Gradually add the granulated white sugar, about 1 tablespoon at a time, whipping until stiff, glossy peaks form. Whip in the vanilla just until blended.

Sift the flour mixture, about one-quarter at a time, over the beaten whites, folding in after each addition just until the flour disappears. Repeat until all the flour mixture is incorporated. Spoon the batter into the tube pan. With a long spatula, gently cut through the batter several times to remove any air pockets.

Bake for 30 to 35 minutes, until the top springs back when lightly touched with a finger. Invert the tube of pan over the neck of an inverted funnel and let the cake cool thoroughly, at least 1½ hours.

To make the glaze, in the top of a double boiler, or in a heatproof bowl over barely simmering water, melt the butter and chocolate, stirring occasionally until smooth. Remove the pan from the heat, but keep the bowl over hot water. Stir in the confectioners' sugar, cinnamon, and 4 tablespoons hot water. Stir until smoothly blended. The glaze should have the texture of thick cream. If it is too thick, gradually stir in enough of the remaining 1 tablespoon hot water to thin. Use warm.

continued

Cake

⅔ cup cake flour

⅔ cup confectioners' sugar

⅓ cup Ghirardelli Unsweetened Cocoa

1½ teaspoons ground cinnamon

12 large egg whites, at room temperature

1½ teaspoons cream of tartar

½ teaspoon salt

½ cup granulated white sugar

1 teaspoon pure vanilla extract

Glaze

¼ cup (½ stick) unsalted butter

2 ounces Ghirardelli 100% Cacao Unsweetened Chocolate baking bar, broken or chopped into 1-inch pieces

1 cup confectioners' sugar

¼ teaspoon ground cinnamon

4 to 5 tablespoons hot water

Run a spatula or long, thin-bladed knife around the pan sides to loosen the cake. Remove the pan sides, then slide a knife along the bottom and center tube of the pan to free the cake. Set the cake, flat side up, on a serving plate. Brush any loose crumbs off the top. Pour the warm glaze over the top of the cake, letting it drizzle over the sides. Let the glaze set for about 30 minutes, or until firm. (If made ahead, store airtight at room temperature up to 3 days.) To serve, cut into slices with a serrated knife.

VARIATION

For a white chocolate glaze, melt 4 ounces Ghirardelli White Chocolate baking bar with 1/2 cup (1 stick) unsalted butter. Glaze as above.

FLOURLESS CHOCOLATE TORTE WITH DARK CHOCOLATE GLAZE

Makes 12 to 16 servings

Preheat the oven to 350°F. Butter the bottom of a 9-inch springform pan. Line the bottom of the pan with parchment paper. Butter the parchment paper.

To make the torte, melt the chocolate and butter in the top of a double boiler or in a heatproof bowl over barely simmering water, stirring occasionally until smooth. Remove from the heat.

Combine the egg yolks, 2 tablespoons of the sugar, the vanilla, and salt in a medium bowl. Beat lightly until well combined. Add the egg mixture to the chocolate, 1 tablespoon at a time, whisking continually.

In a separate bowl, beat the egg whites and the 6 remaining tablespoons of sugar with an electric mixer until soft peaks form. Transfer the chocolate mixture to a large bowl, pour the egg white mixture on top, and carefully fold it in. (Do not overmix.) Spread the batter in the prepared pan.

Bake on the lower shelf of the oven for 30 to 35 minutes, until cracked on top and a tester comes out clean when inserted into the center of the cake. Transfer to a wire rack to cool completely, about one hour. (The cake will shrink down as it cools.) Once cooled, remove the side of the pan

To make the glaze, melt the chocolate and butter in the top of a double boiler or in heatproof bowl over barely simmering water. Stir occasionally until smooth, then remove from the heat. Stir in the milk, syrup, and vanilla.

Place the cake layer (still on the rack) over a baking sheet. When the glaze has cooled, pour it over the center of the cake and let it run down the sides. Use a spatula to smooth the glaze and coat the sides. Decorate the sides of the cake by pressing the nuts into the glaze. Transfer to the refrigerator and allow the glaze to set, about 10 minutes.

Torte

12 ounces Ghirardelli 60% Cacao Bittersweet Chocolate baking bar, broken or chopped into 1-inch pieces

1/2 cup (1 stick) unsalted butter

8 large eggs, separated

1/2 cup granulated white sugar

1 teaspoon pure vanilla extract

Pinch of salt

Chocolate Glaze

4 ounces Ghirardelli Semi-Sweet Chocolate baking bar, broken or chopped into 1-inch pieces

3 tablespoons unsalted butter

1 tablespoon whole milk

1 tablespoon light corn syrup

1/4 teaspoon pure vanilla extract

1/3 cup ground or finely chopped almonds or walnuts

CHOCOLATE CAKES, CUPCAKES, AND TORTES

TRIPLE CHOCOLATE TRUFFLE CAKE

Makes 8 to 12 servings

Created by Gigi Burton, of Plainsboro, New Jersey, this cake won the grand prize of the Ghirardelli Chocolate "Is Your Dessert Intense Enough" contest.

Preheat the oven to 325°F. Arrange a rack in center of oven. Butter the bottom and sides of a 9 by 2-inch round cake pan and line the bottom with parchment paper.

In the top of a double boiler or in a heatproof bowl over barely simmering water, melt the semi-sweet chocolate chips and butter, stirring occasionally until smooth. Cool slightly.

Meanwhile, in a large bowl with an electric mixer fitted with the whip attachment, whip the eggs and salt on medium speed until doubled in volume, about 5 minutes. Gently fold the whipped eggs, a third at a time, into the melted chocolate. Pour the batter into the prepared cake pan. Prepare a water bath for the cake by placing the cake pan in a larger pan and filling the large pan halfway up the sides of the cake pan with hot, but not boiling water.

Bake for about 40 minutes, or until the cake pulls away from the sides of the pan and is set in the center. Remove the pan from the water bath to a cooling rack and cool the cake completely in the pan. Cover with plastic wrap and refrigerate overnight. To remove the cake from the pan, dip the pan in warm water halfway up the sides and run a thin metal spatula around the inside of the pan. Invert onto a plate to unmold and remove the parchment paper.

To prepare the ganache, bring the heavy cream to a simmer in a small saucepan over low heat. Pour the heated cream over the milk chocolate chips. Stir gently until smooth and allow to cool slightly. When the ganache is still warm to the touch, pour over the top of cake and spread with an offset spatula to evenly cover. (There will be some ganache leftover.)

Chill the cake until the ganache sets, about 30 minutes. To garnish, grate the white chocolate bar on top of cake.

3 cups Ghirardelli Semi-Sweet Chocolate Chips

1 cup (2 sticks) unsalted butter, at room temperature

8 large eggs, chilled

1/4 teaspoon salt

1/2 cup heavy cream

1 cup Ghirardelli Milk Chocolate Chips

2 ounces Ghirardelli White Chocolate baking bar, chilled, for garnish

INDIVIDUAL SOFT CENTER CAKES

Makes 4 servings

Preheat the oven to 450°F. Butter four 6-ounce ramekins and dust with sugar.

Melt the butter and chocolate in the top of a double boiler or in a heatproof bowl over barely simmering water, stirring occasionally until smooth.

In a large bowl, whip the whole eggs, egg yolks, sugar, and vanilla with an electric mixer on high speed for about 10 minutes. Fold in the melted chocolate mixture. Fold in the flour just until combined. Spoon the mixture into the prepared ramekins.

Bake for 9 to 10 minutes, until the top and sides are set. The center will be quite soft. Remove from the oven and let sit for about 5 minutes, then unmold each ramekin onto a dessert plate. Serve with a few raspberries and a dollop of whipped cream.

½ cup (1 stick) unsalted butter, cut into pieces

4 ounces Ghirardelli 60% Cacao Bittersweet Chocolate baking bar, broken or chopped into 1-inch pieces

2 large whole eggs

2 large egg yolks

⅓ cup granulated white sugar

½ teaspoon pure vanilla extract

1 tablespoon cake flour

Raspberries or whipped cream, to garnish

FLOURLESS MOCHA TORTE

Makes 8 servings

Preheat the oven to 350°F. Grease two 8-inch or 9-inch round cake pans. Line the bottoms with parchment paper and grease the parchment paper.

To make the torte, melt the bittersweet chocolate in the top of a double boiler or in a heatproof bowl over barely simmering water, stirring occasionally until smooth. Set aside. Dissolve the coffee in the boiling water; set aside.

In a large bowl, whip the egg whites with an electric mixer on medium speed until soft peaks form. Gradually add 1/3 cup sugar and increase the mixing speed to high and continue beating until stiff peaks form.

In another large bowl, whip the yolks, the remaining 1/3 cup sugar, and the salt with an electric mixer on medium speed until thick, about 5 minutes. Slowly add the chocolate mixture and coffee; beat until well blended. Fold one-quarter of the egg whites into the yolk mixture to lighten. Then fold in the remaining whites until no streaks remain. Pour the batter into the prepared pans.

Bake on the center oven rack for 25 minutes. Turn off the oven and leave the cake inside for 5 minutes. Invert and transfer the pans to a wire rack (the centers will fall). Remove the parchment paper and cool completely.

To make the frosting, melt the milk chocolate in the top of a double boiler or in a heatproof bowl over barely simmering water, stirring until smooth. Dissolve the coffee in the boiling water; add all at once to the chocolate, stirring continually until smooth. Cool completely.

In a large bowl, beat the cream at high speed until stiff peaks form. Gently fold the chocolate mixture into the whipped cream.

To assemble the torte, level the top of each layer by cutting off the raised edges with a long serrated knife. Place one layer on a serving plate. Spread the layer with 1 cup of the chocolate whipped cream. Top with the remaining cake layer. Frost the top and sides of the torte with the remaining frosting. Sprinkle the top with bittersweet chocolate shavings.

Torte

6 ounces Ghirardelli 60% Cacao Bittersweet Chocolate baking bar, broken or chopped into 1-inch pieces

1 tablespoon instant freeze-dried coffee

3 tablespoons boiling water

6 large eggs, separated

2/3 cup granulated white sugar

1/4 teaspoon salt

Frosting

4 ounces Ghirardelli Milk Chocolate baking bar, broken or chopped into 1-inch pieces

1 tablespoon instant freeze-dried coffee

1/4 cup boiling water

2 cups heavy cream

1 ounce Ghirardelli 60% Cacao Bittersweet Chocolate baking bar, for shavings (page 19), for garnish '

CHOCOLATE CARAMEL WALNUT TORTE

Makes 12 servings

Preheat the oven to 300°F. Line the bottom of a 9-inch round cake pan or springform pan with a circle of parchment paper. Spray the bottom and sides of the pan with cooking spray. Dust lightly with flour.

To make the torte, in the top of a double boiler or in a heatproof bowl over barely simmering water, melt the chocolate and butter, stirring occasionally until smooth. Cool for 5 minutes.

In a large bowl with an electric mixer or whisk, beat the egg yolks and white sugar until thick; stir in chocolate mixture.

In clean bowl, beat the egg whites until soft peaks form. Stir one-fourth of the egg whites into the chocolate mixture. With a rubber spatula, fold in the remaining egg whites. Spread the batter in the prepared pan.

Bake for 40 minutes, or until the torte is firm to the touch. Cool completely in the pan. Run a small knife around the edge of the pan. Place a wire rack or baking sheet on top of the pan; invert the pan and rack and shake gently to unmold cake. Remove the parchment paper; place a plate on top of cake and invert again; brush off any loose crumbs. Refrigerate.

To make the topping, in a saucepan over medium heat, combine the brown sugar, corn syrup, and butter. Bring to a simmer, whisking to blend. Remove from the heat; stir in the chopped walnuts. Cool at room temperature until gooey but still spreadable. Remove the cake from the refrigerator. Pour the caramel walnut topping onto the cake, spreading just to the edge of the cake with a spatula. Evenly space the walnut halves around the edge of the cake to mark eight pieces. Refrigerate until the topping is firm. Cut the cake into 8 wedges.

Torte

5 ounces Ghirardelli 60% Cacao Bittersweet Chocolate baking bar, broken or chopped into 1-inch pieces

10 tablespoons (1¼ sticks) unsalted butter

4 large eggs, separated

½ cup granulated white sugar

Topping

½ cup firmly packed light brown sugar

½ cup light corn syrup

¼ cup (½ stick) unsalted butter

½ cup chopped walnuts

12 walnut halves

PASSOVER DARK CHOCOLATE VELVET TORTE

Makes 12 servings

If matzo meal is coarse, grind or blend it until finely textured like flour.

Preheat the oven to 350°F. Line the bottom of a 9 by 2-inch round cake pan with parchment paper.

To make the torte, in the top of a double boiler or in a heatproof bowl over barely simmering water, melt the chocolate and margarine, stirring occasionally until smooth. Scrape the chocolate mixture into a large bowl. Stir in the egg yolks and matzo meal.

In a large bowl, whip the egg whites with an electric mixer on high speed until foamy. Gradually add the sugar, whipping until the whites hold stiff, glossy peaks.

Add about one-quarter of the beaten whites to the chocolate mixture; fold to lighten. Add the remaining whites and gently fold until evenly incorporated. Scrape the mixture into the prepared pan and smooth the batter.

Bake for 20 to 25 minutes, until the torte puffs slightly and the center is soft and barely jiggles when the pan is gently shaken.

Cool at least 1 hour in the pan on a rack. (The torte will sink slightly.)

Slide a knife between the torte and the pan to loosen the edges. Set a serving plate over the pan and holding both tightly together, invert. Lift off the pan and the parchment paper. (If made ahead, cover and chill for up to 3 days. Let warm to room temperature at least 1 hour before serving.)

To make the raspberry sauce, purée the berries in a blender. Push the purée through a fine strainer set over a bowl; discard the seeds. Add sugar to taste. (If made ahead, cover and chill for up to 2 days.)

Shortly before serving, sift the cocoa lightly over the torte and garnish with raspberries.

Torte

12 ounces Ghirardelli Semi-Sweet Chocolate baking bar, broken or chopped into 1-inch pieces

3/4 cup margarine (kosher-for-Passover pareve or nondairy, such as Earth Balance Buttery Sticks), cut into 1-inch pieces

6 large eggs, separated

1 tablespoon finely ground matzo meal

1/2 cup granulated white sugar

Ghirardelli Unsweetened Cocoa, for garnish

Fresh raspberries, for garnish (optional)

Raspberry Sauce

4 cups fresh or thawed frozen unsweetened raspberries

5 to 7 tablespoons granulated sugar

CHOCOLATE-ALMOND LAYERED CHEESECAKE

Makes 12 servings

Preheat the oven to 350°. Grease a 9-inch springform pan.

To make the crust, place the almonds on a baking sheet and bake for 3 to 4 minutes, until lightly colored and fragrant. Allow the almonds to cool, then place them in a food processor, and process until finely ground. Combine the crushed wafers, ground almonds, and butter and mix well. Press the mixture onto the bottom of the pan and 1½ inches up the sides. Bake for 8 minutes, then remove to a rack and let cool completely.

To prepare the filling, melt the chocolate in the top of a double boiler, or in a heatproof bowl over barely simmering water, stirring occasionally until smooth.

In a medium-size bowl, beat the cream cheese with an electric mixer on low speed until smooth. Gradually add the sugar and continue beating, scraping down the sides with a rubber spatula. Add the eggs, one at a time, beating well after each addition and scraping down the bowl as needed. With the mixer on low, gradually add the sour cream and salt, beating until just mixed and smooth.

Divide the batter in half. Mix the melted chocolate into one-half of the batter. Pour the chocolate batter into the crust, spreading to create one even layer. Carefully spoon the plain batter on top of the chocolate batter and evenly spread.

Place the pan in the oven and immediately reduce the temperature to 325°F. Bake for 50 to 60 minutes, until the center is just set. Turn off the oven and leave the cake inside for 30 minutes with the oven door closed.

Transfer the cheesecake to a wire rack. Loosen it from the sides of the pan with a metal spatula. Let the cheesecake cool completely, and then chill it for at least 8 hours or overnight. Store covered in the refrigerator for up to 7 days.

Crust

2/3 cup almonds, finely chopped

1¾ cups finely crushed vanilla wafers

1/3 cup (2/3 stick) unsalted butter, melted

Filling

8 ounces Ghirardelli 60% Cacao Bittersweet Chocolate baking bar, broken or chopped into 1-inch pieces

8 ounces cream cheese, at room temperature

1 cup granulated white sugar

3 large eggs

1 cup sour cream

¼ teaspoon salt

CHOCOLATE CHIP CHEESECAKE

Makes 8 servings

Preheat the oven to 350°F. Grease 9-inch springform cake pan.

To make the crust, in a small bowl, mix together the crushed graham crackers, cocoa, and sugar. Stir in the butter. Spoon the mixture into the prepared pan. Press firmly to distribute the crust mixture onto the bottom and halfway up the sides of the pan. Chill the crust while making the filling.

To make the filling, in a medium-size bowl, beat the cream cheese, vanilla, and sugar with an electric mixer at low speed until smooth. Gradually beat in the eggs, increasing the speed slightly as the mixture softens. Beat in the sour cream. Finally, stir in the chocolate chips with a large spoon.

Pour the filling into the chilled crust and set the pan on a baking tray. Bake for 1¼ hours, or until firm. The cheesecake may deflate and crack as it cools, so turn off the oven and let cool slowly in the oven for about 1 hour with the oven door open.

Remove from the oven and let cool completely. Cover and chill in the refrigerator overnight before removing from the pan. Sprinkle the top with grated white chocolate. This cheesecake is best if eaten within 3 days of baking.

Crust

2/3 cup crushed graham crackers

1 tablespoon Ghirardelli Unsweetened Cocoa

¼ cup granulated white sugar

⅓ cup (⅔ stick) unsalted butter, melted

Chocolate Filling

2¼ cups cream cheese, at room temperature

1 teaspoon pure vanilla extract

⅔ cup granulated white sugar

3 large eggs

1 cup sour cream

1 cup Ghirardelli Semi-Sweet Chocolate Chips

2 ounces Ghirardelli White Chocolate baking bar, grated for garnish (optional)

CHOCOLATE ORANGE CHEESECAKE

Makes 8 servings

Preheat oven to 325°F. Grease a 9-inch springform pan.

To make the crust, in a mixing bowl, combine the crushed cookies and butter with a fork. Press the mixture into the bottom and slightly up the sides of the prepared pan. Bake for 15 minutes, then remove from the oven and let cool.

To make the filling, melt the chocolate in the top of a double boiler or in a heatproof bowl over barely simmering water, stirring occasionally until smooth. Remove from the heat.

In a medium bowl with an electric mixer on low speed, beat the cream cheese and sugar until smooth. Add the melted chocolate, juice concentrate, and eggs, one at a time, and beat until just combined. Pour the mixture into the crust.

Bake for 50 minutes. Remove from the oven and let cool for 10 minutes, but do not turn off the oven.

To make the topping, mix the sour cream, sugar, and juice concentrate together. Spread over the still-warm cake. Drizzle the melted chocolate chips over. Bake for 5 minutes. Turn off the heat and cool in the oven with the door slightly open for 30 minutes. Let the cheesecake cool completely, then refrigerate overnight. Store covered in the refrigerator for up to 7 days.

Crust

6 ounces shortbread cookies, crushed

1/4 cup (1/2 stick) unsalted butter, melted

Filling

1 1/2 cups Ghirardelli 60% Cacao Bittersweet Chocolate Chips

16 ounces cream cheese, at room temperature

1 3/4 cups granulated white sugar

1/3 cup orange juice concentrate

3 large eggs

Topping

1 1/2 cups sour cream

6 tablespoons granulated white sugar

2 tablespoons orange juice concentrate

1/4 cup Ghirardelli 60% Cacao Bittersweet Chocolate Chips, melted

CHOCOLATE PIES, TARTS, AND OTHER SPECTACULAR DESSERTS

Chocolate Pecan Pie. 90

Classic Pie Crust 92

Layered Chocolate Pie with Chocolate Curls 93

Chocolate Raspberry Tartlets. 95

Chocolate Ganache Tart 96

Tiramisu 97

Chocolate Pavlova with Milk Chocolate Chip Coffee Cream. 98

Individual Chocolate Soufflés. 100

Chocolate Bread Pudding 102

Mocha Pots de Crème. 103

White Chocolate Crème Brûlée 104

Chocolate Flan 105

White Chocolate Mousse 107

Chocolate Mousse. 108

Luscious Chocolate Ice Cream 109

Individual Chocolate Lava Cakes 110

Ultimate Chocolate Fondue. 113

Hot Fudge Sauce 114

CHOCOLATE PECAN PIE

Makes 8 servings

Preheat the oven to 325°F.

In the top of a double boiler or in a heatproof bowl over barely simmering water, melt the chocolate and butter, stirring occasionally until smooth.

In a large bowl with an electric mixer at medium speed or with a whisk, beat the eggs, corn syrup, brown sugar, vanilla, and salt until blended. Beat in the chocolate mixture. Stir in the pecans and pour into the pie shell.

Place the pie on a baking sheet on the middle rack of the oven and bake for about 55 minutes, or until the filling is set. Cool completely on a rack at room temperature.

4 ounces Ghirardelli Semi-Sweet Chocolate baking bar, broken or chopped into 1-inch pieces

2 tablespoons (1/4 stick) unsalted butter

3 large eggs

1 cup light corn syrup

1/2 cup firmly packed light brown sugar

1 teaspoon pure vanilla extract

1/8 teaspoon salt

1 1/2 cups pecan halves

1 (9-inch) unbaked Classic Pie Crust (page 92) or 1 unbaked ready-made pie crust

CLASSIC PIE CRUST

Makes one 9- or 10-inch pie crust

In a large mixing bowl, stir together the flour and salt. Using a pastry blender, fork, or two knives, cut the shortening and butter into the flour mixture until the mixture has the consistency of small peas. Sprinkle the ice water over the mixture and mix until dough starts coming together, adding more water if necessary.

Using your hands, work the dough gently just until it starts to pull away from the sides of the bowl and can be formed into a 4-inch disk. Wrap and refrigerate the dough for at least 1 hour, or it can be frozen for later use.

For a 9-inch pie, roll out the dough on a lightly floured surface to form a 10-inch circle, about ⅛ inch thick. Roll out the dough into an 11-inch circle to make a 10-inch pie crust. Line the pie plate with the dough. The pastry should extend ⅛ inch beyond the edge of the pie plate. Crimp the edges or press with a fork to create a decorative pattern. Place the pie plate in the refrigerator and chill for 15 minutes.

To bake the crust, preheat the oven to 450°F. Prick the bottom and sides of the crust with the tines of a fork at ½-inch intervals to prevent bubbles from forming while baking. Bake for 8 to 10 minutes, or until light golden brown. Cool on a wire rack.

1 cup all-purpose flour

½ teaspoon salt

⅓ cup solid vegetable shortening

½ tablespoon unsalted butter

2 tablespoons ice water, or more as needed

LAYERED CHOCOLATE PIE WITH CHOCOLATE CURLS

Makes 8 servings

To make the pie, melt the bittersweet chocolate in the top of a double boiler or in a heatproof bowl over barely simmering water, stirring occasionally until smooth.

In a medium bowl, beat the cream cheese with an electric mixer on high speed for 1 minute. Add ½ cup of the cream and the confectioners' sugar and beat for 1 minute. Stir in the melted bittersweet chocolate. Pour the mixture into the pie shell.

Chill in the refrigerator for 1 hour.

Melt the milk chocolate in the top of a double boiler or in a heatproof bowl over barely simmering water, stirring occasionally until smooth.

In a mixing bowl, combine the pudding mix and milk. Beat with an electric mixer on low speed just until blended. Beat on high speed for 2 minutes. Add the melted milk chocolate and continue to beat on high speed for 1 minute. Set aside.

In a small mixing bowl, whip the remaining 1 cup cream until soft peaks form. Fold the whipped cream into the pudding mixture and spread over the cream cheese layer. Chill the pie for 2 hours.

To make the sweetened whipped cream, combine the ½ cup cream and the confectioners' sugar in a bowl and whip until soft peaks form. Transfer the whipped cream to a pastry bag and decorate the pie as desired, with rosettes or just swirls of cream. Alternatively, you can pile the cream on top and smooth out to cover the whole pie. Garnish with chocolate curls and serve.

Pie

4 ounces Ghirardelli 60% Cacao Bittersweet Chocolate baking bar, broken or chopped into 1-inch pieces

8 ounces cream cheese, at room temperature

1½ cups heavy cream

1½ cups confectioners' sugar

1 (9-inch) Classic Pie Crust (page 92) or 1 ready-made pie crust, baked

4 ounces Ghirardelli Milk Chocolate baking bar, broken or chopped into 1-inch pieces

1 (3.4-ounce) package vanilla-flavored instant pudding and pie-filling mix

1¼ cups whole milk

Sweetened Whipped Cream

½ cup heavy cream

2 teaspoons confectioners' sugar

2 ounces Ghirardelli 60% Cacao Bittersweet Chocolate baking bar, formed into curls (page 19), for garnish

CHOCOLATE RASPBERRY TARTLETS

Makes 6 servings

The chocolate pie crust is very versatile and can add an elegant twist to many other pies and tarts. If you'd rather make one large tart, use an 8-inch nonstick tart pan with a removable bottom.

To make the chocolate crust, combine the butter, sugar, and salt in a food processor and process until blended. Add the cocoa and process until smooth. Add the flour and pulse until the mixture is crumbly but can be pinched to hold together. Divide the dough into six equal pieces, flatten each piece into a disk, and wrap in plastic wrap. Refrigerate for at least 30 minutes, or overnight.

Remove one piece of dough at a time from the refrigerator and roll it into a 6-inch circle between two sheets of plastic wrap. If the dough gets too soft, refrigerate until firm before continuing. Remove the top sheet of the plastic wrap; invert the dough circle over a 4½-inch nonstick tartlet pan with a removable bottom. Keeping the plastic wrap on top, press the dough onto the bottom and sides of the pan. Trim any excess dough and carefully peel off the plastic wrap. Repeat with the remaining dough to make six tartlet shells. Refrigerate for at least 30 minutes.

Preheat the oven to 375°F.

Prick the bottoms of the tartlet shells all over with a fork. Bake for 15 minutes, or until the dough looks dry. Allow to cool completely.

To make the chocolate filling, in a medium saucepan over medium heat, bring the cream to a simmer. Remove from the heat and add the chocolate. Let sit for a few minutes to allow the chocolate to melt, then whisk gently until smooth. Cool to room temperature.

Pour ⅓ cup of the chocolate mixture into each tartlet shell. Refrigerate the tartlets at least 1 hour, until the filling is firm. Carefully remove the tartlets from the pans. Arrange the raspberries decoratively on top of the filling.

Chocolate Crust

¾ cup (1½ sticks) unsalted butter, cut into pieces

6 tablespoons granulated white sugar

Pinch of salt

6 tablespoons Ghirardelli Unsweetened Cocoa

1½ cups cake flour

Chocolate Filling

1 cup heavy cream

14 ounces Ghirardelli Semi-Sweet Chocolate Chips

3 cups fresh raspberries

Confectioner's sugar, for dusting

CHOCOLATE GANACHE TART

Makes 8 servings

Preheat the oven to 350°F. Butter the bottom and sides of an 8-inch springform cake pan.

To make the crust, in a medium bowl, stir together the ground wafers and melted butter until the mixture is evenly moist. Transfer to the prepared pan, patting the mixture onto the bottom and three-quarters up the sides of the pan. Bake for about 10 minutes, and then cool completely on a rack.

To make the filling, melt together the chocolate and butter in the top of a double boiler or in a heatproof bowl over barely simmering water, stirring occasionally until smooth. Remove from the heat and let stand for several minutes.

In a medium bowl, mix together the eggs, cream, sugar, salt, and vanilla. Mix in the chocolate mixture and stir until well combined. Pour into the prepared crust. Tap the pan several times on a flat surface to eliminate any air bubbles.

Bake for 20 to 25 minutes, until the filling has risen to an inch from the top of the pan, is set, and has slightly raised in the center. The center will continue to set, then fall slightly as it cools.

Transfer the tart to a rack and let cool completely, about 2 hours. Chill in the refrigerator, uncovered, until the center is firm, about 4 hours. Remove the sides of pan and sprinkle the top of the tart with cocoa.

Crust

1½ cups finely ground chocolate wafer cookies (about 30 wafers)

6 tablespoons (¾ stick) unsalted butter, melted

Ganache Filling

8 ounces Ghirardelli 60% Cacao Bittersweet Chocolate baking bar, broken or chopped into 1-inch pieces

6 tablespoons (¾ stick) unsalted butter, cut into ½-inch cubes

2 large eggs, beaten

½ cup heavy cream

¼ cup granulated white sugar

Pinch of salt

¾ teaspoon pure vanilla extract

Ghirardelli Unsweetened Cocoa, for garnish

TIRAMISU

Makes 15 servings

In a large bowl, beat the mascarpone, 6 tablespoons of the ground chocolate, ¼ cup of the confectioners' sugar, ¼ cup of the liqueur, 1 teaspoon of the vanilla, and the salt with a wire whisk. Set aside.

In a small bowl, beat 1 cup of the cream until stiff peaks form. Fold the whipped cream into the mascarpone mixture.

In another small bowl, combine the remaining ¼ cup liqueur, the remaining ½ teaspoon of vanilla, the water, and the espresso powder.

Line a 2½-quart glass or crystal bowl with one-quarter of the ladyfingers. Brush with 2 tablespoons of the espresso mixture. Spoon one third of the mascarpone mixture over the ladyfingers. Repeat, making 2 more layers of ladyfingers brushed with the espresso mixture and topped with the mascarpone mixture. Top with the remaining ladyfingers, gently pressing them into the mascarpone mixture. Brush the ladyfingers with the remaining espresso mixture. Sprinkle 1 tablespoon of the ground chocolate over the top.

In a small mixing bowl, beat the remaining ½ cup cream and the remaining confectioners' sugar until stiff peaks form. Spoon the whipped cream into a decorating bag with a large star-shaped tip. Pipe large rosettes on top of the dessert. Sprinkle the remaining 2 tablespoons of ground chocolate on the rosettes. Chill for at least 2 hours.

12 ounces mascarpone cheese

½ cup plus 1 tablespoon Ghirardelli Sweet Ground Chocolate & Cocoa

⅓ cup confectioners' sugar

½ cup coffee-flavored liqueur

1½ teaspoons pure vanilla extract

½ teaspoon salt

1½ cups heavy cream

2 tablespoons water

2 teaspoons powdered instant espresso coffee

2 dozen ladyfingers, halved lengthwise

CHOCOLATE PAVLOVA WITH MILK CHOCOLATE CHIP COFFEE CREAM

Makes 6 to 8 servings

The meringues can be piped into four to six individual servings, rather than one large one.

Preheat the oven to 300°F. Line a baking sheet with parchment paper.

To make the meringue, in a large bowl whip the egg whites with an electric mixer at high speed until foamy. Add the cream of tartar and whip until soft peaks form. Add the sugar in a slow steady stream, continuing to whip until the whites are very stiff and the sugar is almost dissolved, about 3 minutes. Fold in the cocoa. The cocoa does not have to be completely incorporated; some streaks are fine. With a rubber spatula, spread the meringue into a 7-inch circle on the baking sheet. Make a slight indentation in the center about 5 inches across. This makes a well for the filling. Bake for 25 minutes. Turn off the oven, but leave the meringue in the oven for 50 minutes to continue to dry out. Remove from the oven and cool to room temperature.

To make the filling, combine the cream, sugar, vanilla, and espresso powder in a large bowl. Whip with an electric mixer at high speed until soft peaks form. Fold in 1/2 cup of the chocolate chips. Spread the cream in the center of the meringue. Dust with the cocoa and sprinkle the remaining chocolate chips on top. Serve immediately.

VARIATION

CHOCOLATE PAVLOVA WITH RASPBERRIES, WHIPPED CREAM, AND MILK CHOCOLATE DRIZZLE FILLING

Bake the meringue as above. Melt chocolate chips in the top of a double boiler or in a heatproof bowl over barely simmering water, stirring until smooth. Spread half the melted chocolate in the center of the meringue. Whip together heavy cream and sugar until soft peaks form. Spread over the melted chocolate. Top with raspberries. Drizzle the remaining melted chocolate on top. Serve immediately.

Meringue

3 large egg whites

1/4 teaspoon cream of tartar

1 cup granulated white sugar

2 teaspoons Ghirardelli Unsweetened Cocoa

Milk Chocolate Chip Coffee Cream Filling

1 cup heavy cream

2 tablespoons granulated white sugar

1 teaspoon pure vanilla extract

1 teaspoon instant espresso powder

1/2 cup Ghirardelli Milk Chocolate Chips, plus extra for garnish

Ghirardelli Unsweetened Cocoa, for dusting

1 cup Ghirardelli Milk Chocolate Chips or Ghirardelli 60% Cacao Bittersweet Chocolate Chips

1/2 cup heavy cream

1 tablespoon granulated white sugar

1 cup fresh raspberries

INDIVIDUAL CHOCOLATE SOUFFLÉS

Makes 2 large or 4 medium servings

Preheat the oven to 350°F. Brush two 1½-cup or four ½-cup ovenproof ramekins with the butter. Dust the bottom and sides of the ramekins with 1 tablespoon of the granulated sugar.

In the top of a double boiler or in a heatproof bowl over barely simmering water, melt the chocolate with the milk and 1 tablespoon granulated sugar, stirring occasionally until smooth. Cool for 5 minutes. Whisk the egg yolk into the chocolate mixture.

In a large bowl with an electric mixer, beat the egg whites at medium speed until soft peaks form. Add the remaining 2 teaspoons granulated sugar and beat until stiff but not dry. With a rubber spatula, fold one-fourth of the egg whites into the chocolate mixture, then fold in the remaining egg whites. Divide among the prepared ramekins. (The soufflés may be prepared ahead up to this point and refrigerated for up to 2 hours. Bake straight from the refrigerator, adding 3 minutes to the baking time.)

Bake large ramekins for 20 minutes; bake small ramekins for 15 minutes. Remove from the oven, then dust the tops of soufflés with confectioners' sugar, and serve immediately.

1 tablespoon unsalted butter, melted

2 tablespoons plus 2 teaspoons granulated white sugar

2 ounces Ghirardelli 60% Cacao Bittersweet Chocolate baking bar, broken or chopped into 1-inch pieces

2 tablespoons plus 2 teaspoons whole milk

1 large egg yolk

2 large egg whites

Confectioners' sugar, for dusting

CHOCOLATE BREAD PUDDING

Makes 12 servings

In a large bowl, whisk together the milk, eggs, butter, and vanilla.

In a small bowl, mix together the sugar, cinnamon, nutmeg, and cocoa. Add to the milk mixture and whisk. Add the bread, raisins, and chocolate chips. Mix well.

Refrigerate for 30 to 60 minutes, until the bread has absorbed most of the liquid.

Preheat the oven to 350°F degrees. Lightly grease a 9 by 13-inch glass baking dish.

Mix the bread pudding once more to evenly distribute the chips and raisins. Pour into the prepared baking dish.

Bake for 1 hour, or until set. Serve the pudding warm, or refrigerate and serve chilled.

4 cups whole milk

4 large eggs

¼ cup (½ stick) unsalted butter, melted

1 tablespoon pure vanilla extract

2 cups granulated white sugar

2 tablespoons ground cinnamon

1 teaspoon ground nutmeg

¼ cup Ghirardelli Unsweetened Cocoa

1 French baguette, cut into cubes (3 to 4 cups)

1 cup raisins

12 ounces Ghirardelli Semi-Sweet Chocolate Chips

MOCHA POTS DE CRÈME

Makes 6 servings

This classic French chocolate dessert gets a boost with a deep coffee flavor.

Bring the cream, sugar, and vanilla to a boil in a saucepan.

Whisk the yolks in a bowl. Whisk about a third of the boiling cream into the yolks. Return the remaining cream to a boil and whisk in the yolk mixture. Continue to cook, whisking constantly, for another 15 to 20 seconds, until slightly thickened. Strain the cream into a bowl and add the chocolate. Whisk until smooth. Whisk in the coffee. Pour into four 5-ounce to 6-ounce pot de crème cups or ramekins. Refrigerate until cooled.

2 cups heavy cream

1 cup granulated white sugar

2 teaspoons pure vanilla extract or 1 vanilla bean, split

6 large egg yolks

6 ounces Ghirardelli 100% Cacao Unsweetened Chocolate baking bar, broken or chopped into 1-inch pieces

½ cup very strong brewed espresso coffee

WHITE CHOCOLATE CRÈME BRÛLÉE

Makes 4 servings

Preheat the oven to 300°F.

In a medium bowl, whisk egg yolks with 1/3 cup sugar until smooth.

In a medium saucepan, bring the cream to a simmer over medium-high heat. Add the white chocolate. Turn off the heat and whisk until the white chocolate is melted. Add 2 tablespoons of the white chocolate mixture to the egg yolk mixture, whisking continually to prevent the eggs from scrambling. Add the remaining white chocolate mixture to the egg yolk mixture. Whisk until smooth. Add the vanilla.

Pour into four 6-inch ramekins or custard cups. Place the cups in a 9 by 13-inch baking pan. Add enough hot water so the cups sit in 1 to 1½ inches of water.

Bake for about 45 minutes, until set. Allow to cool, then refrigerate the custards until chilled. Before serving, sprinkle the tops of each ramekin with 1 teaspoon of sugar and place under the broiler until caramelized, 3 to 4 minutes. Rechill in refrigerator for 5 minutes before serving.

4 large egg yolks, at room temperature

1/3 cup plus 4 teaspoons granulated white sugar

2 cups heavy cream

4 ounces Ghirardelli White Chocolate baking bar, broken or chopped into 1-inch pieces

1/2 teaspoon pure vanilla extract

CHOCOLATE FLAN

Makes 8 servings

Preheat the oven to 300°F.

Combine 1½ cups of the sugar and the water in a saucepan, cover, and bring to a boil over high heat without stirring. When the sugar is completely dissolved and starting to caramelize, remove the lid and continue to boil until the mixture turns a dark amber color, swirling the pan gently so that it colors evenly (do not stir).

Carefully pour the caramel into eight 4-ounce molds, tilting the molds slightly to coat the bottom and sides. Place the molds in a baking dish lined with a clean dish towel.

Pour the remaining caramel onto a silicone baking pan liner or a sheet of lightly oiled aluminum foil. Set aside to cool and harden.

In a saucepan, heat the milk and chocolate to just below a simmer, whisking frequently, until the chocolate is completely melted.

In a bowl, whisk the egg yolks, the remaining ½ cup sugar, the vanilla, and the cinnamon just until mixed; do not overbeat. Slowly whisk in the hot chocolate mixture. Strain into a measuring cup with a spout. Pour into the caramel-coated molds. Pour hot water into the baking dish two-thirds of the way up the sides of the molds. Cover with foil.

Bake for 30 minutes, or until the flan is just set. Remove the molds from the hot water bath and chill.

To serve, run a sharp knife around the edge of each mold, place an upside-down plate on top, invert, and remove the mold. Break up the caramel that has been set aside to cool. The pieces should be small and irregular. Garnish with the caramel shards.

2 cups granulated white sugar

½ cup water

2½ cups whole milk

4 ounces Ghirardelli 60% Cacao Bittersweet Chocolate baking bar, finely chopped

6 large egg yolks

1 teaspoon pure vanilla extract

¼ teaspoon ground cinnamon

WHITE CHOCOLATE MOUSSE

Makes 6 servings

Garnish the mousse with fresh berries to add color and cut through the richness. And, if you don't like orange flavor, substitute raspberry, mint, or coffee liqueur, or ¼ cup water mixed with 1 teaspoon vanilla extract, for the orange liqueur. For an extra special finish, serve the mousse in Chocolate Dessert Cups (page 128).

Melt the chocolate with the liqueur and water in the top of a double boiler or in a heatproof bowl over barely simmering water. Stir gently to blend. Cool until chocolate mixture no longer feels warm to the touch.

In a large bowl with an electric mixer, beat the cream at high speed until soft peaks form. Fold the whipped cream into the chocolate mixture.

In large clean bowl, whisk the egg whites until soft peaks form. With a rubber spatula, fold the egg whites into the chocolate mixture.

Divide the mousse among six dessert bowls or glasses. Chill for at least 1 hour before serving.

8 ounces Ghirardelli White Chocolate baking bar, broken or chopped into 1-inch pieces

¼ cup orange liqueur, such as Grand Marnier

2 tablespoons water

1¼ cups heavy cream

2 large egg whites

CHOCOLATE MOUSSE

Makes 8 to 10 servings

In a large bowl, with an electric mixer at medium-high speed, whip the cream to form light peaks. Set aside in the refrigerator.

Melt the chocolate chips in the top of a double boiler or in a heatproof bowl over barely simmering water, stirring occasionally until smooth.

Meanwhile, whip the eggs with the sugar at medium-high speed for about 10 minutes, until very fluffy and thick.

Stir the coffee into the melted chocolate chips. The mixture will start to thicken, so work quickly. Quickly stir in the beaten eggs, and then fold in the whipped cream. Pour or spoon the mixture into cups or bowls.

Chill until firm, about 2 hours.

2 cups heavy cream

2 cups Ghirardelli 60% Cacao Bittersweet Chocolate Chips

4 large eggs, at room temperature

2 tablespoons granulated white sugar

1/4 cup hot brewed coffee

LUSCIOUS CHOCOLATE ICE CREAM

Makes 1 quart

This ice cream is best if eaten the same day it is made. If it is frozen, let soften in the refrigerator for about 20 minutes before serving.

In a medium bowl, whisk together the egg yolks and sugar; set aside.

In a medium saucepan, heat the cream, milk, and chocolate over medium heat, whisking frequently, until the chocolate melts and the mixture is hot but not boiling. Pour this hot mixture into the egg yolk mixture, whisking constantly, then return the mixture to the pan.

Heat over low heat to 170°F, or until the mixture coats a spoon, stirring constantly. Immediately strain into a bowl and whisk in the vanilla.

Cool the mixture in the refrigerator or cool by setting in a bowl of ice, whisking frequently. Freeze in an ice-cream freezer according to the manufacturer's directions until the ice cream has the consistency of whipped cream. Transfer to a plastic container and store in the freezer.

3 large egg yolks

¼ cup granulated white sugar

1½ cups heavy cream

½ cup whole milk

4 ounces 70% Cacao Extra Bittersweet Chocolate baking bar, finely chopped

½ teaspoon pure vanilla extract

INDIVIDUAL CHOCOLATE LAVA CAKES

Makes 6 servings

To make the centers, in the top of a double boiler or in a heatproof bowl over barely simmering water, melt the 2 ounces of chocolate with the cream. Whisk gently to blend.

Refrigerate for about 2 hours, or until firm. With your hands, form into six balls; refrigerate until needed.

Preheat the oven to 400°F. Spray six 4-ounce ramekins or custard cups with cooking spray.

To make the cakes, in the top of a double boiler or in a heatproof bowl over barely simmering water, melt the 4 ounces of chocolate and the butter, stirring occasionally until smooth.

In a large bowl, with an electric mixer, whisk the whole eggs, egg yolks, sugar, and vanilla on high speed for about 5 minutes, or until thick and light. Fold the melted chocolate mixture and flour into the egg mixture just until combined. Spoon the cake batter into the ramekins. Place a chocolate ball in the middle of each ramekin.

Bake for about 15 minutes, or until the cake is firm to the touch. Remove from the oven and let sit for about 5 minutes. Run a small, sharp knife around the inside of each ramekin, place an upside-down plate on top, invert, and remove the ramekin. Garnish with raspberries and a dollop of whipped cream.

Centers

2 ounces Ghirardelli 60% Cacao Bittersweet Chocolate baking bar, broken or chopped into 1-inch pieces

1/4 cup heavy cream

Cakes

4 ounces Ghirardelli 60% Cacao Bittersweet Chocolate baking bar, broken or chopped into 1-inch pieces

1/2 cup (1 stick) unsalted butter, cut into pieces

2 large whole eggs

2 large egg yolks

1/3 cup granulated white sugar

1/2 teaspoon pure vanilla extract

1/4 cup cake flour

Raspberries and whipped cream, for garnish

ULTIMATE CHOCOLATE FONDUE

Makes 4 to 6 servings

Three types of chocolate make this classic the ultimate chocolate fondue. Dip strawberries, large seedless orange sections, fresh pineapple chunks, pieces of cake, cookies, or any other food you might like to pair with chocolate.

In a medium saucepan, combine the milk, vanilla, and butter. Heat over medium heat until the mixture just simmers. Remove from the heat and stir in the bittersweet and milk chocolates and chocolate liqueur until completely melted and smooth. Serve over a heat source that will keep the fondue warm, but not hot.

1¼ cups whole milk or heavy cream

1 teaspoon pure vanilla extract

2 tablespoons unsalted butter

6 ounces Ghirardelli 70% Cacao Extra Bittersweet Chocolate baking bar, broken or chopped into 1-inch pieces

6 ounces Ghirardelli Milk Chocolate baking bar, broken or chopped into 1-inch pieces

2 tablespoons chocolate liqueur (optional)

HOT FUDGE SAUCE

Makes 2 cups

In a heavy saucepan, combine the chocolate, butter, sugar, water, and corn syrup over medium heat. Stir the mixture continually until the chocolate and butter have melted and the sugar has dissolved. When the sauce comes to a boil, lower the heat and continue boiling gently for 10 minutes. Remove the thickened sauce from the heat and stir in the vanilla. Use immediately or store covered in the refrigerator.

To reheat, place in a small microwave-safe bowl. Microwave on medium power for 6 to 8 minutes, stirring after the first 3 minutes.

4 ounces Ghirardelli 60% Cacao Bittersweet Chocolate baking bar, broken into 1/4-inch pieces

1/4 cup (1/2 stick) butter, cut into pieces

1 1/2 cups granulated white sugar

1/2 cup water

1/4 cup light corn syrup

1 teaspoon pure vanilla extract

CHOCOLATE CANDIES AND BONBONS

Rich Chocolate Fudge. 118

White Chocolate Fudge 119

Dark Chocolate Truffles 120

Milk Chocolate Truffles. 122

White Chocolate Truffles 123

English Toffee. 124

Mendiants. 127

Chocolate Dessert Cups. 128

Chocolate Peanut Butter Bars 130

Chocolate–Almond Berry Bark 132

RICH CHOCOLATE FUDGE

Makes 36 pieces

Line an 8-inch square baking pan with parchment paper.

Combine the chocolate chips, bittersweet chocolate, and condensed milk in the top of a double boiler or a heatproof bowl placed over barely simmering water, stirring occasionally until smooth. Stir in the vanilla and nuts. Spread the fudge evenly in the prepared baking pan. Refrigerate for 2 hours, or until firm. Cut when cool and firm. Store uncovered in the refrigerator.

2 cups Ghirardelli Semi-Sweet Chocolate Chips

2 ounces Ghirardelli 60% Cacao Bittersweet Chocolate baking bar, broken or chopped into 1-inch pieces

1/2 cup sweetened condensed milk

2 1/2 teaspoons pure vanilla extract

1 cup chopped pecans or walnuts

WHITE CHOCOLATE FUDGE

Makes 36 pieces

Line an 8-inch square baking pan with waxed paper. Set aside.

In a large bowl with an electric mixer, beat together cream cheese, sugar, and vanilla at medium speed until smooth.

In the top of a double boiler or in a heatproof bowl placed over barely simmering water, melt the chocolate, stirring occasionally until smooth.

Stir the chocolate into the cream cheese mixture and add the nuts. Spread the mixture in the prepared baking pan.

Chill in the refrigerator until firm, at least 2 hours. Cut into 36 pieces to serve.

8 ounces cream cheese, at room temperature

4 cups confectioners' sugar

1¼ teaspoons pure vanilla extract

12 ounces Ghirardelli White Chocolate baking bar, broken or chopped into 1-inch pieces

1 cup pecans, chopped

DARK CHOCOLATE TRUFFLES

Makes 30 truffles

In a small saucepan, bring the cream to a simmer. Add the butter and stir until melted. Add the chocolate chips. Stir until completely melted and smooth. Remove from the heat and pour into a shallow bowl.

Cool, cover, and refrigerate the mixture until firm, at least 2 hours.

Using a melon baller or small spoon, roll the mixture into 1-inch balls. Roll each ball in the cocoa or nuts. Enjoy immediately or refrigerate in an airtight container for up to 2 weeks

⅓ cup heavy cream

6 tablespoons (¾ stick) unsalted butter, cut into small pieces

2 cups Ghirardelli 60% Cacao Bittersweet Chocolate Chips

⅓ cup Ghirardelli Unsweetened Cocoa or ¾ cup chopped almonds or pecans

MILK CHOCOLATE TRUFFLES

Makes 30 truffles

In a small saucepan, bring the cream to a simmer. Add the butter and stir until melted. Add the chocolate chips. Stir until completely melted and smooth. Remove from the heat and pour into a shallow bowl.

Cool, cover, and refrigerate the mixture until firm, at least 2 hours.

Using a melon baller or small spoon, roll the mixture into 1-inch balls. Roll each ball in the cocoa or almonds. Enjoy immediately or refrigerate in an airtight container for up to 2 weeks.

⅓ cup plus 2 tablespoons heavy cream

½ tablespoon unsalted butter

2 cups Ghirardelli Milk Chocolate Chips

⅓ cup Ghirardelli Unsweetened Cocoa or ¾ cup chopped almonds

WHITE CHOCOLATE TRUFFLES

Makes 30 truffles

In a small saucepan, bring the cream to a simmer. Add the butter and stir until melted. Add the white chocolate. Stir until completely melted and smooth. Remove from the heat and pour into a shallow bowl.

Cool, cover, and refrigerate the mixture until firm, at least 2 hours.

Using a melon baller or small spoon, roll the mixture into 1-inch balls. Roll each ball in the coconut or almonds. Enjoy immediately or refrigerate in an airtight container for up to 2 weeks

1/3 cup plus 2 tablespoons heavy cream

1 tablespoon unsalted butter

8 ounces Ghirardelli White Chocolate baking bar, chopped into small pieces

1 cup shredded coconut or chopped almonds

ENGLISH TOFFEE

Makes 1¼ pounds

Preheat the oven to 350°F. With heavy-duty aluminum foil, form a 10-inch square shell with 1-inch high sides. Place the foil shell on a baking sheet and set aside.

Spread the pecans on a separate baking sheet and toast in the oven for 6 to 8 minutes, or until fragrant.

In a heavy saucepan, cook the butter, sugar, water, and salt over medium heat until the temperature reaches 305°F on a candy thermometer, stirring occasionally. Watch closely after it reaches 290° because the temperature will increase rapidly. Stir in the vanilla and pour the mixture into the foil shell. It will spread but may not reach the edges of the square. Cool at room temperature for 45 minutes, or until hard.

Melt the chocolate in the top of a double boiler or in a heatproof bowl over barely simmering water, stirring occasionally until smooth. Immediately spread the melted chocolate over the cooled toffee and sprinkle with the pecans, pressing lightly to set the pecans into the chocolate. Let set at room temperature for 1 hour, or until the chocolate is set.

Break the toffee into pieces. Store covered at room temperature for up to 1 month.

¾ cup pecans, finely chopped

1 cup (2 sticks) unsalted butter

1 cup granulated white sugar

2 tablespoons water

⅛ teaspoon salt

1 teaspoon pure vanilla extract

8 ounces Ghirardelli 60% Cacao Bittersweet Chocolate baking bar, broken or chopped into 1-inch pieces

MENDIANTS

Makes 16 to 18 candies

These grown-up candies were originally created for Christmas in homage to the colors of the robes of the monastic order. Don't let color stop you, though—choose fruits and nuts that you like, and experiment with other flavor combinations. This recipe is simply a guide.

Preheat the oven to 350°F. Line a baking sheet with parchment paper.

Spread out the nuts in a pie or cake pan. Bake the nuts until golden under the skin, about 8 minutes. Let cool.

Melt the chocolate in the top of a double boiler or in a heatproof bowl over barely simmering water, stirring occasionally until smooth. Working quickly, for each candy, drop 1 teaspoon melted chocolate onto the prepared baking sheet, spacing the drops about 1 inch apart. After you have formed about 6 drops, place a nut, a piece of apricot, and a piece of ginger on each. Repeat to use all the chocolate. If the chocolate becomes too thick to form nice round drops, set the chocolate back over the hot water and stir until chocolate softens, but do not turn on the heat. Remove from the hot water, then continue forming drops. If the chocolate firms before you can attach toppings, dab a little melted chocolate on the back of the topping and place on a chocolate drop.

Let the mendiants stand until firm at room temperature, 5 to 10 minutes. If the chocolate does not firm within 10 minutes, chill until firm, about 10 minutes.

18 pecan halves or whole almonds (1 inch long or smaller)

4 ounces Ghirardelli 60% Cacao Bittersweet Chocolate, Milk Chocolate, or White Chocolate baking bar, broken or chopped into 1-inch pieces

18 pieces (1 by 1/4-inch strips) dried apricots

18 pieces (1 by 1/4-inch strips or 1/4-inch to 1/2-inch chunks) crystallized ginger

CHOCOLATE DESSERT CUPS

Makes 8 dessert cups

Fill these cups with ice cream, sorbet, chocolate mousse, or fresh fruit such as raspberries or strawberries. You will need eight small round balloons to make the cups.

If you are using baking bars, break or chop the chocolate into 1-inch pieces. In the top of a double boiler or in a heatproof bowl over barely simmering water, melt half the chocolate, stirring occasionally until smooth. Cool for about 5 minutes.

Line a baking sheet with parchment paper.

Inflate the balloons to a 4-inch diameter; knot. Holding a balloon by the knot, dip into the chocolate, tipping to cover the balloon halfway up with chocolate. Place the balloon, knotted side up, on the prepared baking sheet, holding the balloon in place until the chocolate starts to set. Repeat with the remaining balloons to make eight cups. Place in the freezer for 5 minutes.

Melt the remaining ¾ pound chocolate and repeat the dipping procedure. Place in the freezer for 10 minutes.

Snip a hole in each balloon to deflate; carefully peel the balloon away from the chocolate. Refrigerate until needed. Use the same day.

VARIATIONS

After dipping, drizzle the cups with a contrasting color of melted chocolate. Or, dip the cups a second time, using a contrasting color of chocolate, leaving part of the first dipping exposed.

1½ pounds Ghirardelli Semi-Sweet, Milk Chocolate, or Classic White Chocolate Chips or baking bars

CHOCOLATE PEANUT BUTTER BARS

Makes about 2 pounds

Pictured on page 133

Butter a 15 by 10-inch baking pan and line with parchment paper.

In the top of a double boiler or in a heatproof bowl over barely simmering water, melt the white chocolate with the peanut butter, stirring occasionally until smooth.

In a second double boiler or in a heatproof bowl over barely simmering water, melt the bittersweet chocolate, stirring occasionally until smooth.

Remove both mixtures from the heat. Pour the peanut butter mixture onto the prepared baking sheet, covering the entire surface of pan. Using a small spoon, drizzle bittersweet chocolate in straight lines over the spread mixture. Using the tip of a small knife, drag through the drizzled bittersweet chocolate to marbleize.

Chill in the refrigerator until firm, at least 2 hours. Cut into small pieces to serve. Keep chilled for up to 2 weeks.

16 ounces Ghirardelli White Chocolate baking bars, broken or chopped into 1-inch pieces

1½ cups chunky peanut butter

6 ounces Ghirardelli 60% Cacao Bittersweet Chocolate baking bars, broken into 1-inch pieces

CHOCOLATE–ALMOND BERRY BARK

Makes 12 to 14 servings

Line a 9 by 13-inch baking pan with parchment paper. Set aside.

In a small skillet, toast the almonds over medium heat, stirring occasionally to promote even cooking, just until golden, about 2 to 3 minutes. Remove from the heat and set aside.

In the top of a double boiler or in a heatproof bowl over barely simmering water, melt the chocolate chips and shortening, stirring until smooth. Remove from the heat and stir in ¼ cup of the toasted nuts and ½ cup of the cranberries. Spread the mixture in the prepared pan, and sprinkle with remaining ¼ cup nuts and ½ cup cranberries. Chill in the refrigerator for at least 30 minutes, or until solid. Break into small pieces to serve.

½ cup chopped almonds

2 cups Ghirardelli Milk Chocolate Chips

1 tablespoon solid vegetable shortening

1 cup cranberries

CLOCKWISE FROM LEFT: Chocolate-Almond Berry Bark,
Hot Fudge Sauce (page 114), Chocolate Peanut Butter Bars
(page 130)

CHOCOLATE BREADS
AND BREAKFAST

Chocolate Panini 136

Chocolate Waffles. 139

Chocolate Banana Crêpes. 140

Buttery Breakfast Scones with Chocolate Chunks 141

Double Chocolate Chip Muffins 142

Double Chocolate Banana Bread 143

CHOCOLATE PANINI

Makes 5 servings (2 sandwiches per serving)

If you prefer your chocolate sweeter, use Ghirardelli Milk Chocolate, or for a more intense treat, try a Ghirardelli 60% Cacao Bittersweet Baking bar.

Slice the bread on the diagonal into slices ½ to ¾ inch thick; there should be at least 20 slices of bread. Break the chocolate into ½ ounce squares. On a 4-ounce bar, there are eight ½-ounce squares. Butter one side of each slice of bread with ½ teaspoon of butter and make a sandwich, butter side out, using a piece and a half of chocolate per sandwich.

Heat a large pan over medium heat and, in batches, cook each sandwich until golden brown, pressing down with a spatula. Flip the sandwiches and cook the second side until golden brown, about 30 seconds. Keep warm in the oven.

Note: These sandwiches can also be made in a panini machine following the manufacturer's instructions.

1 (18-inch) baguette with flaky crust

8 ounces Ghirardelli Semi-Sweet Chocolate baking bars

3 tablespoons unsalted butter, at room temperature

CHOCOLATE WAFFLES

Makes 6 servings

To serve the waffles for dessert, drizzle the waffles with chocolate sauce (see page 140), and garnish with seasonal berries and whipped cream. Otherwise, they are sublime with maple syrup and fresh fruit. They are even delicious served plain.

Preheat a waffle iron according to the manufacturer's directions.

Sift the flour, cocoa, and baking powder into a bowl. Add the sugar and salt and whisk to thoroughly mix. In another bowl, whisk together the milk, egg yolks, and oil. Add to the flour and whisk gently until just combined.

In clean, dry bowl, beat the egg whites with an electric beater at medium speed until they form soft peaks. Fold into the batter and mix in the chocolate chips.

Ladle one-third of the batter onto the center of the waffle iron. Close the top and cook until the waffle is crispy on both sides. Follow the manufacturer's instructions for cooking time. Serve immediately.

2 cups all-purpose flour

1 cup Ghirardelli Unsweetened Cocoa

1 tablespoon baking powder

2 tablespoons granulated white sugar

1/2 teaspoon salt

2 cups whole milk

4 large eggs, separated

4 tablespoons canola oil

1 1/2 cups Ghirardelli Semi-Sweet Chocolate Chips (optional)

CHOCOLATE BANANA CRÊPES

Makes 8 servings

Crêpes can be made ahead of time and stored for up to 2 days in the refrigerator, or wrapped tightly in plastic wrap and frozen for up to 1 month. Thaw in the refrigerator before using.

To make the crêpe batter, combine the milk, eggs, butter, rum, flour, cocoa, and confectioners' sugar in a blender. Blend on high speed for 1 minute, until smooth. Refrigerate for 1 to 12 hours before using.

To make the crêpes, heat a nonstick skillet over medium heat. Dip a paper towel into the canola oil and wipe the pan with the oil. Pour 2 tablespoons crêpe batter into the skillet, swirling to form an even layer. If the batter is too thick to swirl evenly, add more milk or water to thin it out. The crêpes should be thinner than traditional pancakes. Cook the crêpe until the surface is not shiny and the edges are slightly dark, about 2 minutes. Carefully flip the crêpe and cook for 1 minute longer. Remove from the skillet and stack on a plate with a sheet of parchment paper between each crêpe, and cover to keep warm. Repeat to make 16 crêpes.

To make the chocolate sauce, combine the chocolate and cream in a double boiler or in a heatproof bowl over barely simmering water, stirring occasionally until smooth. Keep warm, or reheat before using.

To make the filling, in a large skillet over medium heat, melt the butter with the sugar. Add the bananas and cook until they are warm, about 3 minutes. Remove the skillet from the heat and add the rum. Return the skillet to the heat, tilting carefully to ignite the rum. Shake the pan gently until the flames die out. Alternatively, if you are using an electric stove, cook the rum until reduced by half.

To serve, place 2 crêpes on a plate, add warm bananas, and carefully roll up each of the crêpes. Drizzle with chocolate sauce, add a dollop of whipped cream, and serve immediately.

Crêpes

1 cup whole milk, plus more as needed

2 large eggs

2 tablespoons (¼ stick) unsalted butter, melted

1 tablespoon dark rum

½ cup all-purpose flour

¼ cup Ghirardelli Unsweetened Cocoa

¼ cup confectioners' sugar

Canola oil

Chocolate Sauce

4 ounces Ghirardelli 70% Cacao Extra Bittersweet Chocolate baking bar, broken or chopped into 1-inch pieces

½ cup heavy cream

Banana Filling

¼ cup (½ stick) unsalted butter

2 tablespoons granulated white sugar

6 medium bananas, cut into ½-inch slices

2 tablespoons dark rum

Sweetened whipped cream, for garnish

BUTTERY BREAKFAST SCONES WITH CHOCOLATE CHUNKS

Makes 8 scones

Preheat the oven to 400°F. Line a baking sheet with parchment paper.

To make the scones, in a large bowl, whisk together the flour, baking powder, sugar, and salt until combined. Add the chopped chocolate and stir until mixed. With a pastry blender, cut in the butter.

In a small bowl, stir the heavy cream and egg yolks until slightly blended. Add to the flour mixture and stir with a spoon until the dough just starts to come together. Use your hands to knead the mixture until the dough can be gathered into a moist ball. Do not overknead—the stickiness of the dough is good.

Set the ball on the prepared baking sheet and flatten it to form a round about 8 inches in diameter and 1 inch thick. With a sharp knife, cut the dough into eight wedges (like cutting pieces of a pie), and separate the wedges on the baking sheet about 2 inches apart.

To make the glaze, lightly beat the egg and milk. Using a pastry brush, brush the tops of each scone with the egg and milk mixture and sprinkle with sugar.

Bake the scones for 18 to 20 minutes, until a tester inserted into the center of a scone comes out clean. Transfer the scones still on the parchment paper onto a wire rack and let cool before serving, about 15 minutes. These can be stored for 2 to 3 days.

Scones

2 cups all-purpose flour

1 tablespoon baking powder

1/3 cup granulated white sugar

1/2 teaspoon salt

6 ounces Ghirardelli Semi-Sweet Chocolate baking bars, coarsely chopped

6 tablespoons (3/4 stick) unsalted butter, cut into small cubes

3/4 cup heavy cream

2 large egg yolks

Glaze

1 large egg

1 tablespoon whole milk

2 teaspoons granulated sugar

DOUBLE CHOCOLATE CHIP MUFFINS

Makes 12 muffins

Preheat the oven to 400°F. Line the cups of a muffin pan with paper liners.

In medium bowl, sift together flour, cocoa, baking soda, baking powder, and salt.

In a large bowl with an electric mixer, beat together butter and sugar on medium speed until creamy. Add the eggs and vanilla and beat until light and fluffy. Stir in the sour cream and ¾ cup chocolate chips. Add the flour mixture, stirring just until incorporated.

Spoon the mixture into the muffin cups, filling each cup about three-quarters full. Sprinkle the tops of the muffins with the remaining ¼ cup chocolate chips.

Bake for 20 to 25 minutes, until firm to the touch. Remove the pan from the oven and let stand for 1 to 2 minutes, and then transfer the muffins in their paper cups to a wire rack.

1¾ cups all-purpose flour

½ cup Ghirardelli Unsweetened Cocoa

1 teaspoon baking soda

1 teaspoon baking powder

¼ teaspoon salt

½ cup (1 stick) unsalted butter, slightly softened

½ cup granulated white sugar

2 large eggs, lightly beaten

½ teaspoon pure vanilla extract

1 cup sour cream

1 cup Ghirardelli Semi-Sweet Chocolate Chips

DOUBLE CHOCOLATE BANANA BREAD

Makes two 9-inch loaves

This bread also freezes well, so enjoy one now and save one for later. If you can wait that long . . .

Preheat the oven to 350°F. Lightly grease two 9 by 5-inch loaf pans.

In a large bowl, cream the butter and sugar with an electric mixer on medium speed until fluffy. Beat in the eggs, adding one at a time, and mixing well after each addition. Add the milk and bananas, beating until well blended.

In a separate bowl, whisk together the flour, ground chocolate, baking powder, and salt. Gradually, add the dry ingredients to the creamed mixture. Mix on low only until evenly combined. Stir in the chocolate chips. Pour the batter into the prepared pans.

Bake for 60 to 75 minutes, until golden brown and a tester inserted into the center comes out clean. Set the pans on a rack to cool for 15 minutes, and then turn the loaves out of the pans to cool completely.

¾ cup (1½ sticks) unsalted butter, at room temperature

2 cups granulated white sugar

4 large eggs

½ cup whole milk

4 large ripe bananas, mashed

3½ cups all-purpose flour

1 cup Ghirardelli Sweet Ground Chocolate & Cocoa

1 tablespoon plus 2 teaspoons baking powder

1 teaspoon salt

2 cups Ghirardelli Semi-Sweet Chocolate Chips

ANYTHING-BUT-BORING
CHOCOLATE DRINKS

Grown-Up Hot Chocolate 146

Citrus Sunset™ Hot Chocolate 149

Tiramisu-Me 150

Dark Chocolate Coconut Cooler 151

Dark Chocolate Raspberry Shake. .152

GROWN-UP HOT CHOCOLATE

Makes 4 servings

Instead of flavoring your hot chocolate with amaretto as this recipe calls for, use 1 tablespoon hazelnut, coffee, or orange liqueur, or peppermint schnapps, or 1/2 teaspoon almond or peppermint extract.

In a small saucepan, combine the chocolate chips and half-and-half over low heat and bring to a simmer, whisking constantly. Simmer for 1 minute or until the mixture thickens slightly. Remove from the heat; whisk in the liqueur and vanilla. Pour into four 1/2-cup demitasse or coffee cups. Top each serving with whipped cream and dust with cocoa. Serve immediately.

4 ounces Ghirardelli 60% Cacao Bittersweet Chocolate Chips

1 cup half-and-half

1 tablespoon amaretto

1 teaspoon pure vanilla extract

1/2 cup whipped cream

Ghirardelli 60% Cacao Bittersweet Chocolate Chips or Unsweetened Cocoa, for garnish

CITRUS SUNSET™ HOT CHOCOLATE

Makes 6 servings

You may see small orange pieces that won't dissolve—they are part of the chocolate bars. You can strain them if you wish.

Heat the cream and milk in a heavy-bottomed saucepan over medium heat just until it begins to come to a boil. Remove from the heat and add the chocolate. Let sit for 15 seconds. Add the cocoa and vanilla and whisk until smooth. Serve immediately. The hot chocolate can be reheated.

VARIATION

MINT BLISS HOT CHOCOLATE
Substitute 10½ ounces Ghirardelli Intense Dark Mint Bliss™ bars for the Citrus Sunset™ bars.

2 cups heavy cream

4 cups whole milk

10½ ounces Ghirardelli Intense Dark Citrus Sunset™ bars, coarsely chopped

1 tablespoon plus 1 teaspoon Ghirardelli Unsweetened Cocoa

1 teaspoon pure vanilla extract

TIRAMISU-ME

Makes 4 servings

This recipe was developed for Ghirardelli by Elizabeth Falkner. Rum syrup, a flavored syrup used in coffees, drinks, and baked goods, can be found at most grocery or specialty food outlets. Serve with biscotti.

To make the white chocolate mixture, in a small bowl, mix the mascarpone cheese and white chocolate chips. Set aside in the refrigerator.

To make the ganache, combine the milk, water, and sugar in a saucepan over medium heat and bring just to a boil, stirring. Immediately remove from the heat and with an immersion blender, carefully purée until thickened.

Place the chocolate in a bowl. Pour the milk mixture over the chocolate and let it rest for 2 minutes. Whisk or stir until the mixture is smooth and the chocolate has dissolved. Cover and chill in the refrigerator for 1 hour.

To assemble the drink, set out four tall clear glasses. In each glass, spoon in one-quarter of the mascarpone mixture. Next, spoon in one-quarter of the ganache mixture. Pour in ½ cup of the coffee. Add 3 tablespoons vanilla syrup and 3 tablespoons rum syrup. Top with whipped cream and dust with cocoa.

White Chocolate Mixture

2 ounces (about 5 tablespoons) mascarpone cheese

¼ cup Ghirardelli Classic White Chocolate Chips

Ganache Mixture

½ cup whole milk

2 tablespoons water

1 tablespoon plus 1 teaspoon granulated white sugar

2 ounces 70% Cacao Extra Bittersweet Chocolate baking bar, broken or chopped into 1-inch pieces

2 cups freshly brewed coffee or chilled coffee

¾ cup vanilla syrup

¾ cup rum syrup

Whipped cream, for garnishing

1 tablespoon Ghirardelli Unsweetened Cocoa, for dusting

DARK CHOCOLATE COCONUT COOLER

Makes 2 servings

This recipe was developed for Ghirardelli by Elizabeth Falkner.

Combine the ganache, coconut milk, rum syrup, and ice in a blender and purée until smooth, about 1 minute. Pour into two glasses and sprinkle each with the almonds.

¼ cup Ganache Mixture (page 150)

¼ cup coconut milk

3 tablespoons rum or coconut syrup

2 cups ice

2 tablespoons toasted and crushed almonds

DARK CHOCOLATE RASPBERRY SHAKE

Makes 2 servings

This recipe was developed for Ghirardelli by Elizabeth Falkner.

Combine the raspberry syrup, ice cream, milk, and ice in a blender and purée until smooth, about 1 minute.

In the bottom of each glass, spoon in 2 tablespoons ganache mixture. Pour the raspberry milkshake on top. Garnish each glass with a dark chocolate square.

2 tablespoons raspberry syrup

2 scoops vanilla ice cream

½ cup whole milk

2 cups ice

¼ cup Ganache Mixture (page 150)

2 Ghirardelli Dark Chocolate with Raspberry Filling Squares™, for garnish

ACKNOWLEDGMENTS

The Ghirardelli Chocolate Company would like to thank everyone involved in the development of this cookbook. The production of this collection of indulgent chocolate creations was truly a collaborative effort from professionals, employees, and friends, all of whom played vital roles in the development of this book.

We would like to thank Jennifer Gebert, our Marketing Coordinator, for her countless hours and dedication to this creative work. It is with relentless drive and spirit that she managed everything from recipe development and manuscript writing to photo shoots and final revisions. In addition, we would like to recognize Danielle Jin, our Director of Marketing, for her leadership and direction on this project. Thank you to Fabrizio Parini, Senior Vice President of Marketing, and Andreas Pfluger, CEO of the Ghirardelli Chocolate Company, for their continued support on this book. The Ghirardelli Chocolate Research and Development team deserves special thanks, especially Vicki Wong, Steve Genzoli, Kevin Tamaki, and Carmen Fung. Also thanks to Allison Bhusri, Nia Jusuf, and all of the Ghirardelli employees and friends who helped test and taste recipes.

Thank you to photographer Leigh Beisch and her assistants Lauren Grant and Shana Lopes. Also thanks to food stylist Merilee Bordin and her assistant Nan Bullock, and to prop stylist Emma Star Jensen.

Thank you to Ten Speed Press, especially senior editor Amanda Berne for her expert direction and management, and to publisher Lorena Jones for taking on the project. Thank you also to copyeditor Andrea Chesman, proofreader Leslie Evans, and designer Ed Anderson for bringing it all together.

Thank you to the chefs at Ketchum Food Center for transforming our recipe ideas into a delicious reality.

A special thanks to Elizabeth Falkner, Chef/Owner of Citizen Cake, Citizen Cupcake, and Orson for her creative touch in our drinks chapter.

Lastly and most profoundly, we would like to thank all of our devoted consumers for their passion for chocolate baking and their continued loyalty and support of the Ghirardelli brand.

GLOSSARY

Alkalized Cocoa Powder (Dutch-Processed):
Cocoa powder that has been chemically treated, usually with potassium carbonate, to reduce acidity.

Bloom: Dullness, streaks, graying, or white discoloration on the surface of chocolate, indicating that it has been improperly tempered or stored where there have been temperature fluctuations or moisture. Bloom is unattractive, but not harmful to consume.

Cacao: The defining ingredient in all chocolate and chocolate products. The term "cacao" refers to the tree and its fruit, and the seeds, also known as cocoa beans, inside the fruit, which are processed to make chocolate.

Candy Thermometer: A thermometer that measures a range of temperatures from 40°F to 400°F to allow for accurate heat measurement when making certain candies (fudge, toffee).

Chocolate Liquor: Also known as unsweetened chocolate. Often used in baking, chocolate liquor is pure ground cacao nibs. Despite the name, there is no alcohol in chocolate liquor.

Chocolate Truffle: A rich confection made from chocolate and cream (ganache), although it may contain butter, eggs, and other flavorings. Truffles may be dipped in chocolate or rolled in cocoa powder or both. Although American-style chocolate truffles are larger and may be decorated, the original European chocolate truffle is bite-sized with a rough cocoa-dusted exterior.

Cocoa: The term cocoa is used in different ways. When it appears on a chocolate label with a percentage, it denotes the total cocoa bean (cacao) content of the chocolate, and the term is sometimes used interchangeably with chocolate liquor, cacao, cocoa beans, or cocoa solids.

Cocoa Beans: Chocolate is made from cocoa beans, which are the seeds of the fruit of the cacao tree.

Cocoa Butter: The unique ivory-colored fat that constitutes 50 to 54 percent of roasted cocoa beans. Cocoa butter has little flavor of its own, but it adds considerable richness and depth to the flavor of chocolate. Cocoa butter makes chocolate fluid when melted and crisp when hardened. Chocolate melts readily and luxuriously on the tongue because cocoa butter melts at body temperature. Cocoa butter contributes to the creamy smooth texture and the long finish that characterize fine chocolate.

Cocoa Mass (or Cocoa Masse): An alternate term for the total cocoa bean, cacao, chocolate liquor, or cocoa content of chocolate.

Cocoa Nibs: Pieces of hulled, roasted cocoa beans.

Cocoa Powder: Used as an ingredient in baking or as the base for a hot beverage. Cocoa powder is chocolate liquor, which has been pressed to remove most of its fat, and then pulverized to a powder. High-fat cocoa powders typically contain 22 to 24 percent cocoa butter; low-fat cocoa powders typically contain 10 to 12 percent cocoa butter. "Natural" cocoa powder is cocoa powder that has not been "Dutch-processed" or treated with alkalis.

Cocoa Solids: An alternate term referring to the total cocoa bean or cacao content of chocolate.

Dry or Nonfat Cocoa Solids: The nonfat portion of the cocoa bean.

Ganache: A French word that describes a mixture of chocolate and heavy cream, used in glazing or filling pastries. Both ingredients are heated and then mixed together until the chocolate has completely melted.

Gloss: The satiny sheen or mirror-like shine on the surface of a perfectly tempered piece of chocolate.

Heavy Cream (Heavy Whipping Cream): A cream with a milk-fat content from 36 to 40 percent. It can usually be found in the dairy section at most large grocery stores or gourmet food stores.

Lecithin: A natural emulsifier added to chocolate to promote fluidity when the chocolate is melted. The lecithin used in chocolate manufacture is derived from soy.

Mouthfeel: The texture of a substance in your mouth; how chocolate feels as it melts on your palate.

Notes: The variety of distinctive flavors or hints of flavor that one can pick up when tasting and appreciating an individual piece of chocolate. Chocolate, like fine wine, has a flavor profile that's very individual. It's common to pick up hints of smoke, coffee, cherry, vanilla, nuts, or citrus in chocolate. No two people will necessarily pick up the exact same notes in chocolate, depending on their experience savoring chocolate.

Parchment Paper: A silicone-coated paper that can withstand high heat and is generally used to line baking pans because it does not stick to pastries. Parchment paper can also be used to form pastry bags and can be found in most grocery stores.

Pastry Bag: A cone-shaped bag used in pastry decorating and filling.

Pastry Blender: A small and relatively inexpensive wire tool used to cut butter (or margarine, or shortening) into smaller pieces, into a flour mixture. Using two knifes or a fork can achieve the same results.

Pastry Brush: A brush made of plastic fiber or silicone that is very similar in shape and size to a paint brush. Pastry brushes are generally used to spread glazes on top of the crust or surface of the pastry.

Peaks: Used to refer to the three stages in whipping cream and egg whites to a specific firmness. A soft peak barely holds it shape and can droop down when a spoon or beaters are lifted. A medium peak holds its shape fairly well with the exception of the tip, which curls over into itself when a spoon or beaters are lifted. A firm peak stands straight up and does not curl or droop at the tip when a spoon or beaters are lifted.

Ramekin: An individual baking dish that is 3 to 4 inches in diameter, is generally made of porcelain, and is used for individual crème brulées, soufflés, and other recipes.

Springform Pan: A round, metallic cake pan—usually deeper than a regular cake pan—that has a clamp on the side, which when unlatched, releases the sides of the pan from the bottom. This allows cakes and cheesecakes to be easily removed from the pan and cut.

Water Bath: A shallow container filled with warm water in which a smaller pan of food is cooked (either in the oven or on the stove). The water bath gently cooks mousses and puddings and may be used to keep food warm.

INDEX

A

Almonds
  chocolate-almond berry bark, 132
  chocolate-almond layered cheesecake, 82
  dark chocolate coconut cooler, 151
  dark chocolate truffles, 120
  flourless chocolate torte, 73
  mendiants, 127
  white chocolate truffles, 123
Amaretto, in grown-up hot chocolate, 146
Angel food cake, cinnamon-scented chocolate, 71–72
Appearance of chocolate, 21
Apricots
  chocolate apricot rugelach, 43
  mendiants, 127
Aroma of chocolate, 21–22

B

Banana(s)
  bread, double chocolate, 143
  chocolate banana crêpes, 140
Bars
  chocolate and peanut butter cheesecake, 60
  chocolate peanut butter, 130
  classic blondies, 57
  See also Brownies
Biscotti
  dipping chocolate for, 48
  double chocolate-hazelnut, 46
  marbled, 47

Bittersweet chocolate baking bars
  cherry and white chocolate brownies, 59
  chocolate-almond layered cheesecake, 82
  chocolate caramel walnut torte, 80
  chocolate checkerboards, 37–38
  chocolate flan, 105
  chocolate ganache tarte, 96
  chocolate gingerbread men, 42
  chocolate peanut butter bars, 130
  chocolate pinwheels, 39
  chocolate sauce, 140
  devil's food cake with sinful chocolate frosting, 64
  English toffee, 124
  flourless chocolate torte, 73
  flourless mocha torte, 78
  fudgy chocolate brownies, 53
  hot fudge sauce, 114
  individual chocolate lava cakes, 110
  individual chocolate soufflés, 100
  individual soft center cakes, 76
  layered chocolate pie with chocolate curls, 93
  luscious chocolate ice cream, 109
  mendiants, 127

  milk chocolate chip cookies with pecans, 30
  rich chocolate fudge, 118
  substitutions, 19
  tiramisu-me, 150
  ultimate chocolate fondue, 113
Bittersweet chocolate chips
  chocolate chip cookies, 28
  chocolate mousse, 108
  chocolate orange cheesecake, 86
  dark chocolate truffles, 120
  drizzle filling, 98
  grown-up hot chocolate, 146
  ultimate double chocolate cookies, 32
Black and white macaroons, 44
Blondies, classic, 57
Bonbons. *See* Candies/bonbons
Bread(s)
  banana, double chocolate, 143
  crêpes, chocolate banana, 140
  muffins, double chocolate chip, 142
  panini, chocolate, 136
  pudding, chocolate, 102
  scones, buttery breakfast, with chocolate chunks, 141
Breakfast dishes
  buttery breakfast scones with chocolate chunks, 141
  chocolate waffles, 139
  double chocolate chip muffins, 142

Brownies
  cherry and white chocolate, 59
  chocolate caramel, 56
  classic chocolate, 52
  fudgy chocolate, 53
  peppermint, 54
Butter pecan frosting, 66
Buttery breakfast scones with chocolate chunks, 141

C

Cacao beans, 14
Cakes
  angel food, cinnamon-scented chocolate, 71–72
  devil's food, 64
  German chocolate, 66
  individual chocolate lava, 110
  individual soft center, 76
  triple chocolate truffle, 75
  white chocolate peppermint, 67
  See also Cheesecake(s); Cupcakes; Frostings; Tortes
Candies/bonbons
  chocolate–almond berry bark, 132
  chocolate dessert cups, 128
  chocolate peanut butter bars, 130
  English toffee, 124
  making/dipping, 18
  mendiants, 127
  See also Fudge; Truffle(s)

Caramel
  chocolate brownies, 56
  chocolate walnut torte, 84
Checkerboards, chocolate,
    37–38
Cheesecake(s)
  bars, chocolate and peanut
    butter, 60
  chocolate-almond layered, 82
  chocolate chip, 75
  chocolate orange, 86
Cherry and white chocolate
    brownies, 59
Chocolate
  cacao beans for, 14
  entertaining with, 23–24
  history of, 13
  measurements, 20
  melting methods, 17–18
  pastry garnishes, 19
  production process, 15
  storing, 17
  tasting/appreciation of, 21–22
  tempering, 18
Chocolate-almond berry bark,
    132
Chocolate-almond layered
    cheesecake, 82
Chocolate and peanut butter
    cheesecake bars, 60
Chocolate apricot rugelach, 43
Chocolate banana crèpes, 140
Chocolate bread pudding, 102
Chocolate caramel brownies, 56
Chocolate caramel walnut torte,
    80
Chocolate checkerboards,
    37–38
Chocolate chip cheesecake, 85
Chocolate chip cookies, 28
Chocolate dessert cups, 128

Chocolate-dipped lemon
    cookies, 41
Chocolate flan, 105
Chocolate ganache tart, 96
Chocolate gingerbread men, 42
Chocolate Mexican wedding
    cookies, 35
Chocolate mousse, 108
Chocolate orange cheesecake,
    86
Chocolate panini, 136
Chocolate pavlova with milk
    chocolate chip coffee
    cream, 98
Chocolate peanut butter bars,
    130
Chocolate pecan pie, 90
Chocolate pinwheels, 39
Chocolate raspberry tartlets, 95
Chocolate sauce, 140
Chocolate shortbread cookies,
    39
Chocolate waffles, 139
"Choc-tail" party, 23
Cinnamon-scented chocolate
    angel food cake, 71–72
Citrus Sunset hot chocolate, 149
Classic blondies, 57
Classic chocolate brownies, 52
Classic pie crust, 92
Coatings. See Toppings/coatings
Coconut
  black and white macaroons,
    44
  butter pecan frosting, 66
  dark chocolate coconut
    cooler, 151
  white chocolate truffles, 123
Coffee/espresso
  chocolate checkerboards,
    37–38

chocolate mousse, 108
chocolate pinwheels, 39
cream, milk chocolate chip,
    chocolate pavlova with, 98
dark chocolate cupcakes, 68
flourless mocha torte, 78
mocha pots de crème, 103
tiramisu, 97
tiramisu-me, 150
Cookies
  chocolate
    checkerboards, 37–38
    gingerbread men, 42
    Mexican wedding, 35
    peanut butter, 34
    pinwheels, 39
    shortbread, 36
    ultimate double, 32
  chocolate chip
    milk, Ghirardelli, and var.,
      28
    milk, with pecans, 30
    oatmeal, 31
  lemon, chocolate-dipped, 41
  macaroons, black and white,
    44
  rugelach, chocolate apricot,
    43
  sandwich
    chocolate gingerbread men
      variation, 42
    dipped chocolate, 36
    sugar, double chocolate, 40
  See also Biscotti
Cooler, dark chocolate coconut,
    151
Cranberries, in chocolate-
    almond berry bark, 132
Cream cheese
  chocolate-almond layered
    cheesecake, 82

chocolate and peanut butter
    cheesecake bars, 60
chocolate chip cheesecake, 85
chocolate orange cheesecake,
    86
layered chocolate pie with
    chocolate curls, 93
white chocolate fudge, 119
Cream, milk chocolate chip
    coffee, chocolate pavlova
    with, 98
Cream, whipped, 98
  sweetened, 93
Crème brûlée, white chocolate,
    104
Crème, mocha pots de, 103
Crêpes, chocolate banana, 140
Crusts
  for chocolate-almond layered
    cheesecake, 82
  for chocolate and peanut
    butter cheesecake bars, 60
  chocolate, for chocolate
    raspberry tartlets, 95
  for chocolate ganache tarte,
    96
  for chocolate orange
    cheesecake, 86
  pie, classic, 90, 92, 93
Cupcakes
  dark chocolate, 68
  white chocolate, 70
Curls, chocolate, 19
  layered chocolate pie with, 93

D
Dark chocolate coconut cooler,
    151
Dark chocolate cupcakes, 68
Dark chocolate glaze, 77

Dark chocolate raspberry shake, 152

Dark chocolate truffles, 120

Dark chocolate velvet torte, Passover, 81

Dark chocolate with raspberry filling squares, in dark chocolate raspberry shake, 152

Dark chocolate with white mint filling squares, in peppermint brownies, 54

Dessert cups, chocolate, 128

Devil's food cake with sinful chocolate frosting, 64

Dipped chocolate sandwich cookies, 36

Dipping chocolate, for biscotti, 48

Double chocolate banana bread, 143

Double chocolate chip muffins, 142

Double chocolate cookies, ultimate, 32

Double chocolate-hazelnut biscotti, 46

Double chocolate sugar cookies, 40

Drinks
dark chocolate coconut cooler, 151
dark chocolate raspberry shake, 152
tiramisu-me, 150
See also Hot chocolate

E

English toffee, 124

Entertaining, 23–24

Espresso. See Coffee/espresso

F

Flan, chocolate, 105

Flavor of chocolate, 22

Flourless chocolate torte with dark chocolate glaze, 73

Flourless mocha torte, 78

Fondue, ultimate chocolate, 113

Frostings
butter pecan, 66
for dark chocolate cupcakes, 68
for flourless mocha torte, 78
sinful chocolate, 64
white chocolate, 85
for white chocolate cupcakes, 70

Fudge
rich chocolate, 118
sauce, hot, 114
white chocolate, 119

Fudgy chocolate brownies, 53

G

Ganache
chocolate ganache tart, 96
in dark chocolate coconut cooler, 151
in tiramisu-me, 150

Garnishes, chocolate, 19

German chocolate cake, 66

Ghirardelli Chocolate Company
chocolate production process at, 15
chocolate varieties, 16
history of, 11–13
product substitutions, 19–20

Ghirardelli, Domingo, 10–12

Ghirardelli, Domingo, Jr., 12

Ghirardelli milk chocolate chip cookies, 28

Ghirardelli Square, 12–13

Gingerbread men, chocolate, 42

Ginger, in mendiants, 127

Glazes
for chocolate-dipped lemon cookies, 41
for cinnamon-scented angel food cake, 72–73
dark chocolate, for flourless chocolate torte, 73
for double chocolate sugar cookies, 40

Graham crackers
chocolate and peanut butter cheesecake bars, 60
chocolate chip cheesecake crust, 85

Grown-up hot chocolate, 146

H

Hazelnuts
double chocolate-hazelnut biscotti, 46
marbled biscotti, 47

Hot chocolate
Citrus Sunset™, 149
grown-up, 146
Mint Bliss, 149

Hot fudge sauce, 114

I

Ice cream
luscious chocolate, 109
vanilla, in dark chocolate raspberry shake, 152

Individual chocolate lava cakes, 110

Individual chocolate soufflés, 100

Individual soft center cakes, 76

Intense Dark Citrus Sunset™ bars, in Citrus Sunset™ hot chocolate, 149

Intense Dark Mint Bliss™ bars, in Mint Bliss hot chocolate, 149

L

Lava cakes, individual chocolate, 110

Layered chocolate pie with chocolate curls, 93

Lemon(s)
Chocolate-dipped lemon cookies, 41
white chocolate cupcakes, 70

Luscious chocolate ice cream, 109

M

Macaroons, black and white, 44

Marbled biscotti, 47

Mascarpone cheese
in tiramisu, 97
tiramisu-me, 150

Measuring chocolate, 20

Melting chocolate, 17–18

Mendiants, 127

Meringues, 98

Mexican wedding cookies, chocolate, 35

Milk chocolate baking bars
chocolate and peanut butter cheesecake bars, 60
chocolate apricot rugelach, 43
chocolate dessert cups, 128
flourless mocha torte frosting, 78
layered chocolate pie, 93
mendiants, 127
sinful chocolate frosting, 64
ultimate chocolate fondue, 113

Milk chocolate chip(s)
chocolate-almond berry bark,
132
classic blondies, 57
cookies, Ghirardelli, 28
cookies, with pecans, 30
cream, milk chocolate chip
coffee, 98
dark chocolate cupcake
frosting, 68
drizzle filling, 98
milk chocolate truffles, 122
triple chocolate truffle cake,
75
Milk chocolate truffles, 122
Milk chocolate with caramel
filling squares, in chocolate
caramel brownies, 56
Mint Bliss hot chocolate, 149
Mocha
pots de crème, 103
torte, flourless, 78
Mousses
chocolate, 108
white chocolate, 107
Muffins, double chocolate chip,
142

O
Oatmeal chocolate chip cookies,
31
Orange juice/zest
chocolate orange cheesecake,
86
marbled biscotti, 47
white chocolate mousse, 107

P
Panini, chocolate, 136
Passover dark chocolate velvet
torte, 81

Pavlovas
chocolate, with milk
chocolate chip coffee
cream, 98
chocolate, with raspberries,
whipped cream, and milk
chocolate drizzle filling, 98
Peanut butter
chocolate and peanut butter
cheesecake bars, 60
chocolate cookies, 34
chocolate peanut butter bars,
130
Peanuts, in peanut butter
chocolate cookies, 34
Pecans
butter pecan frosting, 67
chocolate apricot rugelach, 43
chocolate Mexican wedding
cookies, 35
chocolate pecan pie, 90
dark chocolate truffles, 120
English toffee, 124
Ghirardelli milk chocolate
chip cookies, 28
mendiants, 127
milk chocolate chip cookies
with, 30
rich chocolate fudge, 118
white chocolate fudge, 119
Peppermint
brownies, 54
white chocolate peppermint
cake, 67
Pie crust, classic, 92, 93
Pies
chocolate pecan, 90
layered chocolate, 93
Pinwheels, chocolate, 37–38
Pots de crème, mocha, 103
Pudding, chocolate bread, 102

R
Raisins, in chocolate bread
pudding, 102
Rapallo (Italy), 10
Raspberry(ies)
chocolate pavlova with
whipped cream, milk
chocolate drizzle filling,
and, 98
chocolate raspberry tartlets,
95
sauce, 81
shake, dark chocolate, 152
Rich chocolate fudge, 118
Rugelach, chocolate apricot, 43
Rum
chocolate banana crêpes, 140
dark chocolate coconut
cooler, 151
syrup, in tiramisu-me, 150

S
Sauces
chocolate, for chocolate
banana crêpes, 140
hot fudge, 114
raspberry, 81
Scones, buttery breakfast, with
chocolate chunks, 141
Semi-sweet chocolate baking
bars
buttery breakfast scones with
chocolate chunks, 141
chocolate apricot rugelach, 43
chocolate dessert cups, 128
chocolate-dipped lemon
cookies, 41
chocolate panini, 136
chocolate pecan pie, 90
classic chocolate brownies, 52

dark chocolate cupcake
frosting, 68
dark chocolate glaze, 77
dipped chocolate sandwich
cookies, 36
double chocolate-hazelnut
biscotti, 46
German chocolate cake, 66
Passover dark chocolate
velvet torte, 81
substitutions, 19
Semi-sweet chocolate chips
black and white macaroons, 44
chocolate bread pudding, 102
chocolate chip cheesecake, 85
chocolate chip cookies, 28
chocolate raspberry tartlets,
95
chocolate waffles, 139
classic blondies, 57
classic chocolate brownies, 52
dark chocolate cupcake
frosting, 68
dipping chocolate, for
biscotti, 48
double chocolate banana
bread, 143
double chocolate chip
muffins, 142
marbled biscotti, 47
oatmeal chocolate chip
cookies, 31
peanut butter chocolate
cookies, 34
rich chocolate fudge, 118
triple chocolate truffle cake,
75
ultimate double chocolate
cookies, 32
Shake, dark chocolate raspberry,
152

Shavings, chocolate, 19
Shortbread cookies, chocolate, 39
Sinful chocolate frosting, 64
Soufflés, individual chocolate, 100
Storing chocolate, 17
Sugar cookies, double chocolate, 40
Sweet ground chocolate & cocoa
  chocolate and peanut butter cheesecake bars, 60
  chocolate caramel brownies, 56
  chocolate Mexican wedding cookies, 35
  double chocolate banana bread, 143
  double chocolate-hazelnut biscotti, 46
  double chocolate sugar cookies, 40
  substitutions, 19–20
  tiramisu, 97

T
Tart, chocolate ganache, 96
Tartlets, chocolate raspberry, 95
Tastings, chocolate, 23–24
Tempering chocolate, 18
Texture of chocolate, 22
Tiramisu, 97
Tiramisu-me, 150
Toffee, English, 124
Toppings/coatings
  for chocolate caramel walnut torte, 80
  for chocolate Mexican wedding cookies, 35

for chocolate orange cheesecake, 86
  See also Frostings; Glazes
Tortes
  chocolate caramel walnut, 80
  flourless chocolate, 77
  flourless mocha, 78
  Passover dark chocolate velvet, 81
Triple chocolate truffle cake, 75
Truffle(s)
  cake, triple chocolate, 83
  dark chocolate, 120
  milk chocolate, 122
  white chocolate, 123

U
Ultimate chocolate fondue, 113
Ultimate double chocolate cookies, 32
Unsweetened chocolate baking bars
  cinnamon-scented chocolate angel food cake glaze, 72–73
  mocha pots de crème, 103
  peppermint brownies, 54
  substitutions, 19–20
Unsweetened cocoa
  angel food cake, 72–73
  chocolate bread pudding, 102
  chocolate checkerboards, 37–38
  chocolate chip cheesecake crust, 85
  chocolate gingerbread men, 42
  chocolate pinwheels, 39
  chocolate raspberry tartlet

crust, 95
  chocolate shortbread cookies, 39
  chocolate waffles, 139
  Citrus Sunset™ hot chocolate, 149
  crêpes, 140
  dark chocolate cupcakes, 68
  dark chocolate truffles, 120
  devil's food cake, 64
  dipped chocolate sandwich cookies, 36
  double chocolate chip muffins, 142
  in meringues, 98
  milk chocolate truffles, 122
  substitutions, 19

V
vanilla pudding/pie mix, in layered chocolate pie, 93
vanilla syrup, in tiramisu-me, 150

W
Waffles, chocolate, 139
Walnuts
  chocolate apricot rugelach, 43
  flourless chocolate torte, 73
  Ghirardelli milk chocolate chip cookies, 28
  oatmeal chocolate chip cookies, 31
  rich chocolate fudge, 118
  torte, chocolate caramel, 84
  ultimate double chocolate cookies, 32
White chocolate baking bars
  cherry and white chocolate

brownies, 59
  chocolate dessert cups, 128
  chocolate peanut butter bars, 130
  cinnamon-scented chocolate angel food cake glaze var., 73
  classic blondies, 57
  mendiants, 127
  triple chocolate truffle cake, 75
  white chocolate crème brûlée, 104
  white chocolate cupcake frosting, 70
  white chocolate frosting, 85
  white chocolate fudge, 119
  white chocolate mousse, 107
  white chocolate truffles, 123
White chocolate chips
  tiramisu-me, 150
  white chocolate cupcakes, 70
White chocolate crème brûlée, 104
White chocolate cupcakes, 70
White chocolate fudge, 119
White chocolate mousse, 107
White chocolate peppermint cake, 67
White chocolate truffles, 123